WILD FLOWERS
OF GREAT BRITAIN
EUROPE, AFRICA & ASIA

WILD FLOWERS
OF GREAT BRITAIN
EUROPE, AFRICA & ASIA

A COMPREHENSIVE GUIDE TO PLANTS AND HOW TO IDENTIFY THEM,
INCLUDING DATA FOR MORE THAN 260 WILD FLOWERS AND FLORA,
ILLUSTRATED WITH OVER 860 MAPS, DRAWINGS AND PHOTOGRAPHS

MICK LAVELLE

southwater

This edition is published by Southwater
an imprint of Anness Publishing Ltd
Hermes House, 88–89 Blackfriars Road
London SE1 8HA; tel. 020 7401 2077; fax 020 7633 9499

www.southwaterbooks.com; www.annesspublishing.com

If you like the images in this book and would like to
investigate using them for publishing, promotions or
advertising, please visit our website
www.practicalpictures.com for more information.

UK agent: The Manning Partnership Ltd
tel. 01225 478444; fax 01225 478440
sales@manning-partnership.co.uk

UK distributor: Grantham Book Services Ltd
tel. 01476 541080; fax 01476 541061
orders@gbs.tbs-ltd.co.uk

North American agent/distributor: National Book Network
tel. 301 459 3366; fax 301 429 5746; www.nbnbooks.com

Australian agent/distributor: Pan Macmillan Australia
tel. 1300 135 113; fax 1300 135 103
customer.service@macmillan.com.au

New Zealand agent/distributor: David Bateman Ltd
tel. (09) 415 7664; fax (09) 415 8892

Publisher: Joanna Lorenz
Editorial Director: Helen Sudell
Editor: Simona Hill
Illustrators: Anthony Duke, Peter Barrett, Penny Brown
and Stuart Jackson-Carter
Production Controller: Steve Lang

A CIP catalogue record for this book is available from the
British Library.

Previously published as part of a larger volume, *The
World Encyclopedia of Wild Flowers and Flora*

CONTENTS

WHAT IS A WILD FLOWER?

The question of what a wild flower is seems steeped in controversy. Purists argue that they must be native to that area, and conservationists often demonize introduced species, despite their having become naturalized and essentially "growing wild".

Flowers are generally considered to be "wild" if they grow without someone having planned where they should be planted. We think of wild flowers as growing in their natural state, with no interference from us, but if we consider the wild species that spring up in gardens, backyards, streets and fields the picture becomes more complex. These plants are indeed wild but thrive in habitats created by humans. In fact, despite every attempt to interfere with their growth, they may well continue to plague farmers, gardeners and city maintenance teams.

Wild flowers are plant species that are at home in a particular place, whether their habitat is natural or the result of human intervention. In any location, from high mountain pastures to great forests, some plants will prosper and others do less well. Each pretty wild flower is the result of countless generations of plants that have striven to exist against staggering odds to ensure that their evolutionary "line" will survive into the future. Some flowers have become highly adapted in order to grow

Above: Traditional meadows are home to many showy species of wild flower.

in these places. They may be dependent not only upon their surroundings but upon other plants, for example by providing shelter from weather, or a stem to scramble through; and even dependent upon animals for their survival, for example, to help spread seed or promote root growth by grazing. Many strange and wonderful plant species have been shaped by their homes, their weather and other inhabitants of their habitat into the perfect form for survival.

It is the showiest flowers that we tend to spend most time looking at – how easily we walk past myriad delicate wild flowers to gaze at one large bloom. Every time we walk across a grassy patch we may carelessly crush hundreds of flowering plants

Left: Plants of deciduous woodland, like these bluebells, grow, flower and set seed before the leaf canopy excludes the light in summer.

Above: Shady banks and overgrown roadsides often harbour a rich variety of species that have disappeared from the surrounding area.

underfoot. They are everywhere and many deserve a closer look. A detailed inspection of even the commonest wayside flower reveals an intricacy and beauty that the work of human hands can rarely approach. Wild flowers are among nature's loveliest gifts: carefree and simple, abundant and serendipitous, they provide an ever-changing panorama of colours, shapes, sizes and textures. It is precisely the informal spontaneity of wild flowers – the random mingling of colours and species, and the way that they change through the seasons – that delights us.

The natural floral jewellery that adorns so much of the Earth's surface has enraptured scientists, artists and writers throughout our history, yet it is easy to forget the true depth of this bounty. Its richness is what this book is all about. All flowering plants – even the tiniest ones – deserve our attention, and to understand them fully we must look both closely and carefully. Describing the wonders of just one flower could fill a whole book; to attempt to include here all the flowering plants in the Eurasia

and Africa would be impossible. This book aims to present a selection: it could be described as a "look through the keyhole" at a world more beautiful than can easily be comprehended. Many plants have had to be omitted and perhaps some of your own favourites are missing. Hopefully, however, you will be inspired to go out and take a fresh look at wild flowers and marvel over these truly remarkable phenomena growing all around us.

Below: Even close-mown or grazed turf may harbour an abundance of small yet colourful wild flower species.

HOW FLOWERS LIVE

Flowering plants are the most diverse and widely studied group in the plant kingdom. They are found all across the Earth's surface, wherever plants have learned to live. From mountaintops and the high Arctic to lush tropical forests, flowers are a familiar feature of every landscape. This wide range of habitats has led to flowers assuming a huge diversity of form. In some cases, the flowers have become so reduced as to be insignificant when compared to the plant as a whole. In others, however, the plant itself may hardly be noticed until it produces a huge flower that seems to arrive from nowhere.

Flowers have even driven the process of evolution, harnessing an army of helpers that include almost every conceivable form of land or air living creatures to help with every phase of their reproductive cycle. Many of the showiest flower types trade rich, nutritious, sugary nectar in return for the services of the "diner" in cross fertilization. Flowers are the courtship vessels of plants and are often highly adapted to receive the attention of just a few creatures, some of which are adapted solely to exploit the food source. Others use a variety of tricks and even entrapments to fulfil this need and yet others have abandoned the need for animals, preferring the wind to do the job for them.

Even once the seed is fertilized, the relationship of many species with animals does not end. There are a whole range of ingenious methods by which they recruit animals into spreading their seed for them, and by doing this they not only guarantee the survival of future generations but may also spread the offspring far and wide from the parent plants.

Left: The vivid colours of wild flowers are designed to attract pollinators but have also long attracted the attention of humans.

HOW PLANTS ARE CLASSIFIED

In an attempt to understand the world, humans have become fascinated with the classification of every aspect of it. While such classifications are useful to us, they do not naturally occur in nature and are at best approximations of the true nature of diversity.

Classification helps us to recognize millions of individual species of plants. In pre-literate times plant recognition was a practical necessity, since eating the wrong plants could be fatal.

The earliest written record of a system of plant classification can be attributed to Theophrastus (*c*.372–287BC), a student of Plato and Aristotle, to whom even Alexander the Great sent plant material that he encountered on his expeditions. In his *Enquiry into Plants* and *On the Causes of Plants*, Theophrastus included the classification of species into trees, shrubs, subshrubs and herbs, listing about 500 different plants; he also made a distinction between flowering and non-flowering plants.

The binomial system

The shift toward modern systems of classification began at the time of the Renaissance in Europe (1300–1600). Improvements in navigation, which opened up the world and enabled plants to be collected from much further afield, coincided with the invention of the printing press, which meant information about the new

discoveries could be published widely. Interest in plants increased enormously, and by the 17th century the number of known species was becoming too high to manage without a classification system. The British naturalist John Ray is credited with revising the concept of naming and describing organisms. However, most were classified using a whole string of words that resembled a sentence rather than a name. During the 18th century, the Swedish botanist Carl von Linné (1707–78), who published his work under the Latinized form of his name, Carolus Linnaeus, created a referable system of nomenclature that became the foundation of the system used today. He is often cited as the father of modern taxonomy, or hierarchical classification.

Linnaeus chose to use Latin, then the international language of learned scholars, which enabled scientists speaking and writing different native languages to communicate clearly. His system is now known as binomial

Below: Primula vulgaris, the primrose gets its genus (first) name from the Latin primus referring to its early appearance in spring.

Above: The rose has been highly bred, and many of the types now in cultivation bear little resemblance to wild types. The genus name Rosa, *is the original Latin name for the plant.*

nomenclature (from *bi* meaning "two", *nomen* meaning "name" and *calatus* meaning "called"). Each species is given a generic name – something like a surname – and a specific name, the equivalent of a personal or first name. We still use this system, which has been standardized over the years, for naming and classifying organisms.

The generic (genus) name comes first, and always starts with a capital letter. It is followed by the specific (species) name, which is always in lower case. This combination of genus and species gives a name that is unique to a particular organism. For example, although there are many types of rose in the genus *Rosa*, there is only one called *R. rubiginosa* – commonly known as the sweet briar. (These names are italicized in print.)

The names of plants sometimes change. Name changes usually indicate reclassification of plant species, often as a result of advances in molecular biology. For example, the

Chrysanthemum genus has recently been split into eight different genera, including *Dendranthema*, *Tanacetum* and *Leucanthemum*. It may take the botanical literature years to reflect such changes, and in the meantime inconsistencies in the printed names of plants can appear.

Plant families

Another useful way of classifying plants is by family. Many families are distinctive in terms of their growth characteristics and preferences, while others are very large and diverse, including numerous different genera. There are 380 families of flowering plants, containing all the species known to science that have already been classified. The largest family is the Asteraceae (aster family), which contains 1,317 genera and 21,000 species. In contrast, some plant families are very small: an example is the Cephalotaceae, or saxifragales family, of which a single species, *Cephalotus follicularis*, is found growing along a small stretch of coast in western Australia.

As our understanding increases, and more species are discovered and classified, there is sure to be intense debate over the placement of new and existing species within families.

Below: Geranium *(shown here) is often confused with the closely related genus* Pelargonium *due to Linnaeus (mistakenly) classifying both as* Geranium *in 1753.*

Above: Ferns and mosses represent an ancient lineage of plants that do not produce flowers or seed and as such, are classified as lower plants.

*Below: Salad burnet (*Sanguisorba minor*) is a small herbaceous plant in Rosaceae, yet at first glance it does not appear even remotely similar to the woody genus* Rosa.

THE ORIGIN OF SPECIES

The earliest flowering plants appeared on Earth around 350 million years ago in the ancient carboniferous forests, although they really began their "takeover" of the planet 120 million years ago, when the dinosaurs ruled the world.

The first flowers were probably quite insignificant by current standards, but their appearance, coupled with their ability to produce a protective fruit around the seed, marked the beginning of a new era. Despite their rather low key entrance in the early Cretaceous period, by the time the dinosaurs met their end some 55 million years later, most of the major flowering plant groups had already appeared.

Two distinct ways of life emerged for flowering plants. Some continued to reproduce as they had always done – letting the wind control whether pollen from one flower met another flower of the same type. Others, however worked in harmony with insects and other animals, which they enticed with sweet nectar and large, colourful flowers. The relationship was very successful and led to the almost infinite variety of forms and colours that we see around us in plants today.

Below: 500 million years ago non-vascular plants such as hornworts, liverworts, lichens, and mosses grew on Earth.

The first living things

The Earth is around 4.5 billion years old, and life is estimated to have begun around 3.75 billion years ago: for around 750 million years the Earth was (as far as we know) lifeless. It was a hostile environment, with a surface hot enough to boil water and an atmosphere that would have been poisonous to us, yet life is likely to have begun as soon as the surface was cool enough for water to lie on its surface. It was not life as we know it – more a thick soup of chemicals than the miracle of creation – but it was life. This was the situation for 500 million years, until a strange twist of fate assured the rise of the plants.

Primitive single-celled bacteria, which we now know as cyanobacteria, evolved from the existing life forms. They probably appeared remarkably similar to their counterparts, but with one spectacular difference. These cells

Below: 425 million years ago seedless vascular plants such as club mosses, early ferns and horsetails became evident.

were able to take carbon dioxide (which was then very abundant in the Earth's atmosphere) and water and convert them into sugar (an energy-rich food) and oxygen. The effect would have been barely noticeable at first, but over a period of a few hundred million years it changed the atmosphere from one rich in carbon dioxide to one that was at one point almost one-third oxygen. Over this time many of the formerly dominant species died out, but the plant-like bacteria gained the ascendance.

Despite this, plants remained water-bound for another 2.5 billion years. It was not until 425–500 million years ago (a date that is still hotly contested) that they made their first tentative appearance on land. The earliest forms were very simple in comparison to modern plants, but their descendants still exist and probably look similar in many respects – mosses and liverworts

Below: 200 million years ago seeded vascular plants such as the gymnosperms, seed ferns, conifers, cycads and ginkgoes thrived.

are the best examples. The first advance that we know of was marked by the appearance of a plant called *Cooksonia*, 430 million years ago. Within 70 million years, species had diversified and evolved to form lush tropical forests; despite being relatively new to the land, plants had made up for lost time in spectacular style.

The fossil record

Evidence of early plants has been found in the fossil record. As mud and other sediments were deposited, forming rocks, pieces of living organisms were deposited with them. Surviving as fossils, these give us an extraordinary picture of what the Earth was like at any one time. In addition, the chemistry of the atmosphere and hydrosphere (the oceans, rivers, lakes and clouds) of the time can be determined by analysis of the rock. These signs allow us to piece together the story and understand how plants have changed over time.

Darwin's theory of evolution

In 1859, the British naturalist Charles Darwin published *On the Origin of Species*. The work caused a stir at the

Below: 120 million years ago recognizable species of seeded vascular plants, such as magnolias and water lilies evolved.

time as it opposed conventional Church doctrine. Darwin argued that the Earth had been created not tens of thousands of years ago (as the Church claimed) but billions of years ago. The idea was seen as revolutionary or even heretical, but in fact it reflected a growing school of thought that recognized that animal and plant species could change over time. Darwin's grandfather had written on the topic, and Darwin himself acknowledged 20 predecessors who had added to the subject. His original contribution, however, was to sift through this increasing body of evidence and combine it with his own observations during his travels around the world from 1831 to 1836.

Darwin determined that single species, through environmental influence, were able to change over time to suit their surroundings. These changes happened not within the lifetime of an individual organism but through the inheritance of characteristics that were valuable in aiding survival and competing with other organisms for the essentials of life. Though he did not then understand the mechanism by which this happened, Darwin concluded that all modern species have evolved through the process of natural

Above: Though it is a modern species, this Magnolia *flower is very similar to the earliest flower forms of 120 million years ago.*

selection, or "survival of the fittest". The theory revolutionized the study of biology and his work remains a cornerstone of evolutionary science.

Since Darwin's time, the body of evidence has grown. There is still much that we do not know, but many evolutionary scientists believe that there are more species on the planet today than at any time in its entire history. We now mostly understand how changes are passed on to offspring and have been able to piece together an evolutionary hierarchy, where we can see when plants first appeared and how they have changed over time.

Below: Today there are more species of flowering plants in the world than there ever have been at any other time.

THE PARTS OF A PLANT

While plants have undergone many individual changes over millions of years, most of them still have features in common. Flowering plants generally possess roots, stems, leaves and, of course, flowers, all of which may be useful in identifying them.

Learning to recognize species is essentially a question of simple observation combined with knowledge of plant structure. This is because all modern flowering plants have evolved from a common ancestry – just as most mammals, birds and reptiles possess one head, four limbs, up to five toes per leg and sometimes a tail, because they are all variants of a prior design.

Even when plants have become highly specialized, the common features still persist, albeit in a modified form, and this often betrays a relationship between species that appear unrelated.

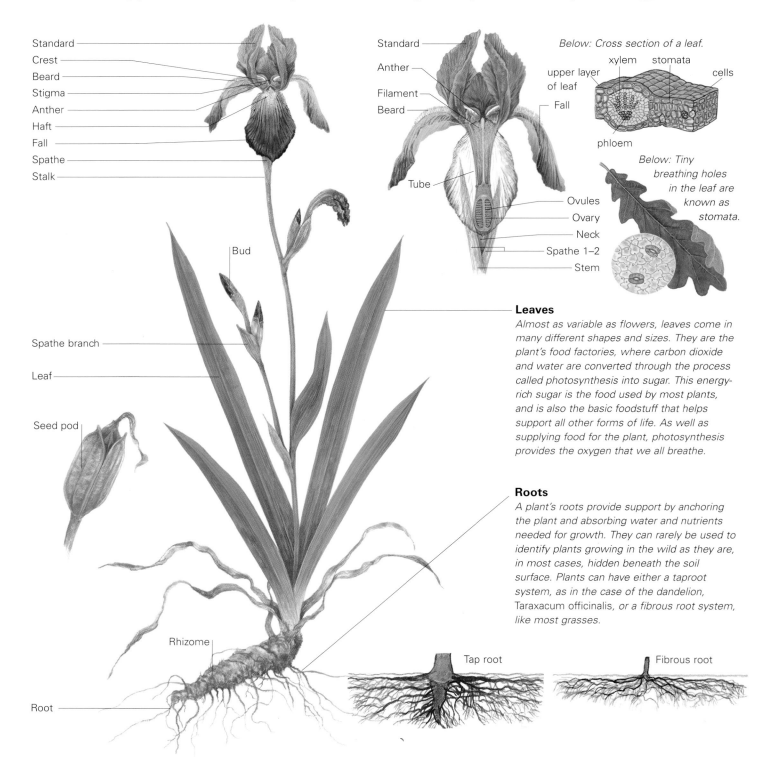

Standard
Crest
Beard
Stigma
Anther
Haft
Fall
Spathe
Stalk

Bud

Spathe branch

Leaf

Seed pod

Rhizome

Root

Standard
Anther
Filament
Beard
Tube
Fall
Ovules
Ovary
Neck
Spathe 1–2
Stem

Below: Cross section of a leaf.

upper layer of leaf
xylem
stomata
cells
phloem

Below: Tiny breathing holes in the leaf are known as stomata.

Tap root

Fibrous root

Leaves

Almost as variable as flowers, leaves come in many different shapes and sizes. They are the plant's food factories, where carbon dioxide and water are converted through the process called photosynthesis into sugar. This energy-rich sugar is the food used by most plants, and is also the basic foodstuff that helps support all other forms of life. As well as supplying food for the plant, photosynthesis provides the oxygen that we all breathe.

Roots

A plant's roots provide support by anchoring the plant and absorbing water and nutrients needed for growth. They can rarely be used to identify plants growing in the wild as they are, in most cases, hidden beneath the soil surface. Plants can have either a taproot system, as in the case of the dandelion, Taraxacum officinalis, or a fibrous root system, like most grasses.

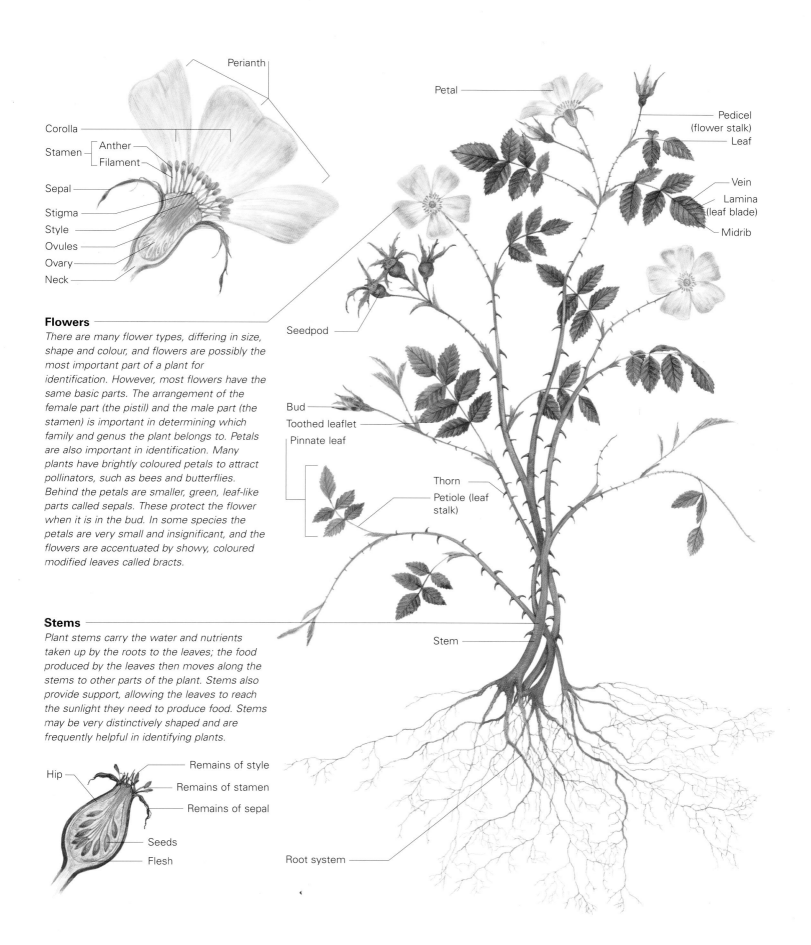

Perianth

Corolla

Stamen — Anther
— Filament

Sepal

Stigma

Style

Ovules

Ovary

Neck

Petal

Pedicel
(flower stalk)

Leaf

Vein

Lamina
(leaf blade)

Midrib

Seedpod

Bud

Toothed leaflet

Pinnate leaf

Thorn

Petiole (leaf
stalk)

Stem

Flowers

There are many flower types, differing in size, shape and colour, and flowers are possibly the most important part of a plant for identification. However, most flowers have the same basic parts. The arrangement of the female part (the pistil) and the male part (the stamen) is important in determining which family and genus the plant belongs to. Petals are also important in identification. Many plants have brightly coloured petals to attract pollinators, such as bees and butterflies. Behind the petals are smaller, green, leaf-like parts called sepals. These protect the flower when it is in the bud. In some species the petals are very small and insignificant, and the flowers are accentuated by showy, coloured modified leaves called bracts.

Stems

Plant stems carry the water and nutrients taken up by the roots to the leaves; the food produced by the leaves then moves along the stems to other parts of the plant. Stems also provide support, allowing the leaves to reach the sunlight they need to produce food. Stems may be very distinctively shaped and are frequently helpful in identifying plants.

Hip

Remains of style

Remains of stamen

Remains of sepal

Seeds

Flesh

Root system

LEAF FORMS AND SHAPES

While leaves vary considerably in appearance, all are basically similar in terms of their internal anatomy. Leaves are the factories within which plants produce their own food, although in some plants, they have become highly adapted and may fulfil a variety of other roles.

Leaves are able to breathe: air passes freely in and out through specialized pores known as stomata, which are usually found on the lower leaf surface, or epidermis. The stomata can be opened and closed by the plant to regulate water evaporation. This is crucial as it allows the plant to cool down, preventing damage through overheating, though the leaves of some plants (those in dry climates) have few stomata in order to conserve water. Leaves also contain vascular tissue, which is responsible for transporting water to the leaves and food from the leaf to other parts of the plant. The veins are easily visible on both the surface and the underside of most leaves. The same types of tissue are present in the plant's stems and collectively they form a continuous link from root tip to leaf tip.

Leaf fall

When leaves have finished their useful life the plant sheds them. Deciduous trees and shrubs shed all their leaves annually and enter a dormant phase, usually in the autumn in temperate areas or immediately preceding a dry season in warmer climates, to avoid seasonal stresses such as cold or excessive heat damage. Herbaceous

Above: Cacti live in very harsh dry conditions and have leaves that are reduced to small spiny pads.

plants (also known as herbs) and other non-woody plants normally lose all of their top growth, including the leaves, for similar reasons. Many plants of the arctic, temperate and dry regions fall into this category.

Plants that do not shed all their leaves at once are said to be evergreen. These plants ride out harsh conditions but may also enter a dormant phase where no new growth commences until conditions improve. Evergreen plants also shed leaves, but tend to do so all through the year, particularly during active growth periods. Many tropical plants fit into this category.

Leaf modifications

Leaves are arguably the most highly modified of all plant organs, and show a vast diversity of form and function. Flower petals are thought to have arisen from leaves. The adaptations in leaves often reflect ways in which

plants have changed in order to cope with specific environmental factors in their natural habitats.

Cactus spines are an example of an extreme leaf modification. The spines are part of a modified leaf called an areole. They are in fact modified leaf hairs, and the small furry base of the spine, or spine cluster, is all that remains of the leaf itself. Cacti and some other succulents have altered so that the stem is the main site of food production, and the leaves have adopted a defensive role.

Other leaf modifications include the development of tendrils to help plants climb, coloured bracts around flowers to attract potential pollinators, and – the most celebrated – traps that attract and ensnare insects to supplement the plant's mineral requirements.

Leaf shape

Leaves grow in a tremendous variety of sizes and shapes, which can be useful in helping to identify the plant.
• Leaf margins, or edges, occur in a variety of forms. The simplest is a smooth, continuous line, which is described as "entire". Often, however, the edge is broken up in a definite pattern, such as "serrated" or "lobed".
• The apex, or leaf tip, may vary in shape, even between closely related species. This may reflect environmental factors. The base of the leaf is also variable and is considered along with the way the leaf is attached to the stem.
• Veination may form an identifiable trait. Monocotyledonous plants have parallel veins that run the length of the leaf. Dicotyledonous plants have a netted arrangement that is complex.
• Leaves can be categorized as simple or compound. A simple leaf is one single leaf blade on a stalk. Compound leaves are made up of a group of leaflets, with a single stalk, attaching the group to the stem.

Leaf arrangements

How leaves are attached or arranged on a stem can be a useful tool in plant identification.

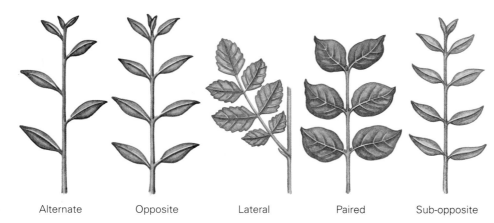

Alternate   Opposite   Lateral   Paired   Sub-opposite

Leaf shapes

Leaves are almost as varied as flowers in respect of their shapes, although they offer less of a clue as to the relationships *between even quite closely related species. Similar shapes, sizes and colours of leaf may occur on quite unrelated species and it is* *thought that this is mainly due to the original environmental circumstances that a plant evolved within.*

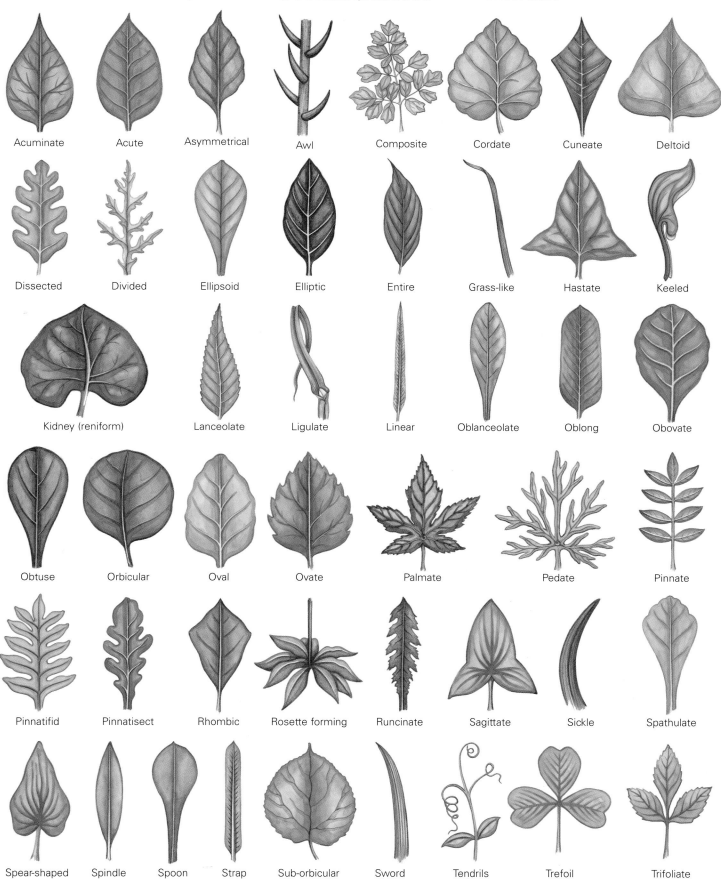

Acuminate · Acute · Asymmetrical · Awl · Composite · Cordate · Cuneate · Deltoid

Dissected · Divided · Ellipsoid · Elliptic · Entire · Grass-like · Hastate · Keeled

Kidney (reniform) · Lanceolate · Ligulate · Linear · Oblanceolate · Oblong · Obovate

Obtuse · Orbicular · Oval · Ovate · Palmate · Pedate · Pinnate

Pinnatifid · Pinnatisect · Rhombic · Rosette forming · Runcinate · Sagittate · Sickle · Spathulate

Spear-shaped · Spindle · Spoon · Strap · Sub-orbicular · Sword · Tendrils · Trefoil · Trifoliate

FLOWERS AND FLOWER FORMS

A flower is the reproductive organ of plants classified as angiosperms – plants that flower and form fruits containing seeds. The function of a flower is to produce seeds through sexual reproduction. The seeds produce the next generation of a species and are the means by which the species is able to spread.

It is generally thought that a flower is the product of a modified stem, with the petals being modified leaves. The flower stem, called a pedicel, bears on its end the part of the flower called the receptacle. The various other parts are arranged in whorls on the receptacle: four main whorls make up a flower.

• The outermost whorl, located nearest the base of the receptacle where it joins the pedicel, is the calyx. This is made up of sepals (modified leaves that typically enclose the closed flower bud), which are usually green but may appear very like petals in some flowers, such as narcissus.

• The next whorl is the corolla – more commonly known as the petals. These are usually thin, soft and coloured, and are used to attract pollinators such as insects.

• The androecium (from the Greek *andros* and *oikia*, meaning "man's house") contains the male flower parts, consisting of one or two whorls of stamens. Each stamen consists of a filament topped by an anther, where pollen is produced.

• The last and innermost whorl is the gynoecium (from the Greek *gynaikos*

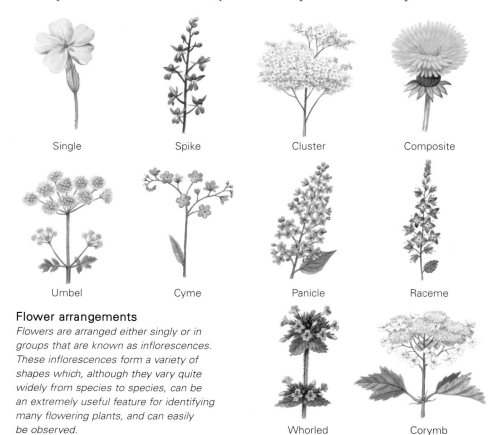

Single   Spike   Cluster   Composite

Umbel   Cyme   Panicle   Raceme

Whorled   Corymb

Flower arrangements
Flowers are arranged either singly or in groups that are known as inflorescences. These inflorescences form a variety of shapes which, although they vary quite widely from species to species, can be an extremely useful feature for identifying many flowering plants, and can easily be observed.

Flower shapes
Flowers display a wide variety of shapes that may be the result of individual flowers or the close arrangement into a flower-like compound inflorescence.

and *oikia*, meaning "woman's house"), which consists of a pistil with one or more carpels. The carpel is the female reproductive organ, containing an ovary with ovules. The sticky tip of the pistil – the stigma – is where pollen must be deposited in order to fertilize the seed. The stalk that supports this is known as the style.

This floral structure is considered typical, though many plant species show a wide variety of modifications from it. However, despite the differences between genera, most flowers are simply variations on a theme and a basic knowledge of their arrangement is all you really need to get started with their identification.

Bell   Tulip-shaped   Cupped   Domed   Star-shaped   Funnel   Goblet

Pea-like   Saucer   Conical   Flattened   Tubular   Urn-shaped

Monoecious and dioecious plants

In most species, the individual flowers have both a pistil and several stamens, and are described by botanists as "perfect" (bisexual or hermaphrodite). In some species, however, the flowers are "imperfect" (unisexual) and possess either male or female parts only. If each individual plant has either only male or only female flowers, the species is described as dioecious (from the Greek *di* and *oikia*, meaning "two houses"). If unisexual male and female flowers both appear on the same plant, the species is described as monoecious (from the Greek *mono* and *oikia*, meaning "one house").

Attracting pollinators

Many flowers have evolved specifically to attract animals that will pollinate them and aid seed formation. These commonly have nectaries – specialized glands that produce sugary nectar – in order to attract such animals. As many

Different growing habits

Plants exhibit a variety of growing habits, often reflecting the type of habitat or niche they have specifically evolved to occupy. These are often important features to note when identifying a plant as the flowers may not be present all year round. The growing habits shown below describe all of the flowers that are featured in this directory.

Above: Flowers that attract bees will often have petals that form a wide surface for landing and copious amounts of nectar.

pollinators have colour vision, brightly coloured flowers have evolved to attract them. Flowers may also attract pollinators by scent, which is often attractive to humans – though not always: the flower of the tropical rafflesia, for example, which is pollinated by flies, produces a smell like that of rotting flesh.

There are certain flowers whose form is so breathtaking as to render them almost unnatural to our eyes. Flowering plants such as orchids have developed a stunning array of forms and many have developed intricate relationships with their pollinators. Flowers that are pollinated by the wind have no need to attract animals and therefore tend not to be showy.

Above: Flowers whose petals form a protective cup or tube are especially attractive to butterflies or other insects with long mouthparts.

Types of inflorescence

Some plants bear only one flower per stem, called solitary flowers. Many other plants bear clusters of flowers, which are known as inflorescences. Most inflorescences may be classified into two groups, racemes and cymes.

In a raceme, the individual flowers making up the inflorescence bloom progressively from the bottom of the stem to the top. Racemose inflorescences include arrangements called spike, raceme, corymb, umbel and head. In the cyme group, the top floret opens first and the blooms continue to open downward along the peduncle, or inflorescence stalk. Cymes may be simple or compound.

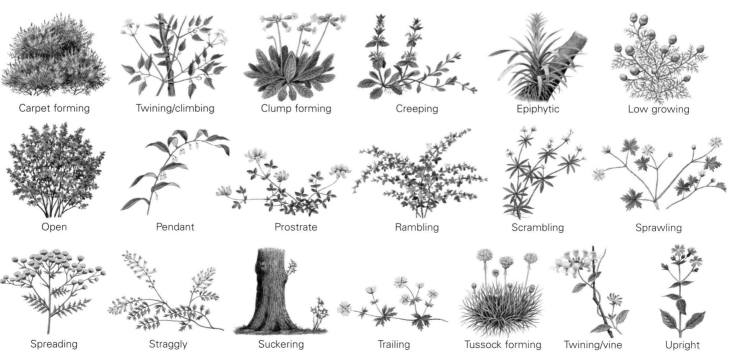

Carpet forming   Twining/climbing   Clump forming   Creeping   Epiphytic   Low growing

Open   Pendant   Prostrate   Rambling   Scrambling   Sprawling

Spreading   Straggly   Suckering   Trailing   Tussock forming   Twining/vine   Upright

THE LIFE CYCLE OF FLOWERING PLANTS

All flowering plants, from giant forest trees that live for thousands of years to the most ephemeral desert annuals that live for only a few weeks, follow the same pattern of life. Their lifespan, size, apparent durability and survival strategies vary considerably, but they have much in common.

Above: Field poppy, Papaver rhoeas, *is an annual that completes its life cycle in one season.*

Above: Wild carrot, Daucus carota, *is a biennial that grows one year and flowers the next.*

Above: Yellow flag, Iris pseudacorus, *is a perennial that lives and flowers for many years.*

All flowering plants begin life as seeds. These are in essence tiny, baby plants that have been left in a state of suspended animation with enough food to support them in the first few days of their new life. In order to grow, seed must be viable (alive). It is a misconception that seed is not living. It is and, like all living things, has a life-span. However, many types of seed can remain dormant for decades, waiting for the right opportunity to commence their cycle of growth and development.

Eventually, the seed will be triggered into germinating by the right combination of moisture, temperature and a suitable soil or growing medium.

Some seeds have specific needs; proteas and banksias must be exposed to smoke to prompt germination, and many berries, such as mistletoe, need to be exposed to the stomach acid of an animal. In most cases, the germinating plant is totally reliant on the energy stored in the seed until it pushes its growing tip above the soil.

The maturing plant

Once above ground the stem grows up toward the light and soon produces leaves that unfold and begin to harvest light energy. As the stems grow upward the plant also extends its roots down into the soil, providing stability and allowing the plant to harvest both water and minerals that are vital to its growth.

Once the plant reaches its mature phase of growth, changes in its internal chemistry enable it to begin flowering. When this happens depends upon the species, but many plants – except those with the briefest life cycles – continue to grow while they produce flower buds. These buds develop into flowers, which are pollinated by the wind or by pollinators such as bees, moths or other animals.

Once a flower has been pollinated, it will usually fade quickly before turning into fruit, as the fertilized

Yearly life cycle of herbaceous plants
All flowering plants begin life as a seed. Some grow and flower within the first season, while others grow for several years before they flower. Herbaceous plants whether annual or perennial, grow and flower before dying back down at the end of the season.

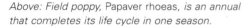

ovary swells and the new seeds develop. The seeds will continue to develop within the fruit until the embryos are fully mature and the seeds are capable of growing into new plants. This may be very quick in the case of small herbs, but in some shrubs and trees it can take two or more seasons for the seeds to develop fully.

Plants may take just one season to reach flowering stage, or may live for many years before they flower. Once flowering begins, certain species flower repeatedly for many seasons, some lasting decades or even centuries. There is much variability between species, but most plants follow one of three main types of life cycle.

Annuals

Plants that live for a single growing season, or less, are called annuals. Their life cycle is completed within a year. In this time the plant will grow, flower, set fruit containing seeds, and die. Many common flowering plants adopt this strategy which has the advantage of allowing them to colonize areas quickly and make the best of the available growing conditions.

Biennials

Plants that need two growing seasons to complete their life cycle are known as biennials. Generally, biennials germinate and grow foliage in the first growing season before resting over the winter. In the second growing season the plant enters a mature phase, in which it flowers, sets fruit and then dies. A biennial flowers only once before dying. A few plants may grow only foliage for several years before finally flowering and dying.

Perennials

All the remaining plant types live for three or more years, and may go on growing, flowering and producing fruit for many years. Some perennial species may take a number of years to grow to flowering size, but all of them are characterized by a more permanent existence than that of annuals and biennials.

Life cycle of a dandelion

Above: The flower begins life as a tight bud that opens from the tip to reveal the yellow petals of the tiny individual flowers.

Above: As the flower opens further, it widens and flattens in order to make a perch for the bumblebees, which are its pollinators.

Above: Once the flower has been pollinated, it closes up again and the plant commences the process of seed production.

Above: Once the seed is ripened, the flower bracts re-open, and the parachute-like seed appendages (achenes) spread to form a globe.

Above: As the ripened seed dries, it is easily dislodged and is carried away from the parent plant by even a light breeze.

Above: Once the seed has been dispersed, the flower stalk is redundant and quickly withers, leaving only the leafy rosette.

WHAT IS POLLINATION?

Before a flower can develop seeds for reproduction it must be pollinated: pollen must be moved from the male anthers to the female stigma. There are many ways that flowers can be pollinated, but each species is designed to be pollinated in a specific way.

Some flowers are able to self-pollinate – when pollen from their own anthers is deposited on the stigma – but for most, pollination needs some outside help. Wind moves the pollen for some plants, of which grasses are a prime example, but others require the assistance of an animal pollinator. These move pollen from the anthers to the stigma of a flower, and also often carry it between different flowers or plants of the same species. Many animals are known to be good pollinators but those that most commonly perform this task include bees, butterflies, hummingbirds, moths, some flies, some wasps and nectar-feeding bats.

The benefits of pollination

Plants benefit from pollinators because the movement of pollen allows them to set seed and ultimately begin a new generation. The pollinators, however, are not acting for the benefit of the plant. For them, pollination is an incidental by-product of their efforts to collect nectar and/or pollen from flowers for themselves or their own offspring. In evolutionary terms it is a perfect example of two unrelated species gradually adapting to mutual dependence, where both benefit from

Below: Pollinators, such as this swallowtail butterfly, feed upon the energy- and protein-rich nectar while pollinating the plant.

the relationship. Indeed, many plants have become so dependent on a particular pollinator that their flowers have become specifically adapted to favour them. The loss of the pollinating animal from a habitat may ultimately result in the extinction of the plant as well.

Fertilization

Once a pollen grain has landed on the stigma, it must reach the ovaries of the flower in order to fuse with the female cell and begin to form a seed. It does this by germinating and growing a long thin tube that reaches down the style into the flower's ovaries. The pollen tube provides a pathway for the male chromosomes to reach the egg cell in the ovule. One pollen grain fertilizes one egg cell, and together they form the new seed.

Flower forms and pollinators

Plants that are wind-pollinated often have flowers that are small, numerous and inconspicuous. They produce huge amounts of pollen, which saturates the air around them to ensure that some reaches nearby plants.

Plants pollinated by bees usually have yellow or blue flowers that are sweetly fragrant and produce sweet nectar. Bees tend to visit flowers whose petals form a wide enough surface for them to land upon. As they take the nectar the visiting bees are dusted with pollen, which is brushed off on the next flowers they visit.

Some plants are pollinated by beetles. Their flowers are usually white or dull in colour, mostly with yeasty, spicy or fruity odours. They may or may not produce nectar, as pollen is often the source of food that they seek.

Flowers that rely on fly pollination usually possess flowers that are dull red or brown and have foul odours: in some cases this may be accompanied

Fertilization

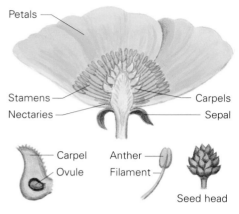

Above: In this buttercup the male flower parts (stamens, each comprised of an anther and a filament) are laden with pollen and surround ovule (egg) containing female parts (carpels).

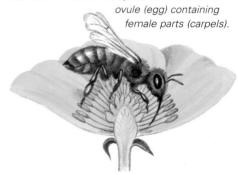

Above and below: Bees tend to visit flowers whose petals form a wide enough surface for them to land upon. As they take the nectar the bees are dusted with pollen, which brushes on to the flowers they visit next.

Once a pollen grain has landed on the stigma, it must reach the ovaries of the flower in order to fuse with the female cell and begin to form a seed. It does this by germinating and growing a long thin tube that reaches down the style into the flower's ovaries. The pollen tube provides a pathway for the male chromosomes to reach the egg cell in the ovule. One pollen grain fertilizes one egg cell, and together they form the new seed.

Above: Bees need a flat landing platform on which to rest before collecting pollen from plants.

by nectar that resembles (in taste and smell) rotting meat.

Butterflies mainly pollinate flowers that are relatively long and tubular in shape – although this can vary considerably – while moths typically pollinate flowers that are yellow or white and fragrant, as they visit them at night.

Some plants are pollinated by birds, though they are far fewer than those visited by insects. Plants that attract hummingbirds, for example, have brightly coloured flowers but very little fragrance, since the birds have no sense of smell. All bird-pollinated flowers are similar in structure to those pollinated by butterflies, in that they have a long tubular shape, but they produce even greater amounts of nectar.

Self-pollination and cross-pollination

While it is possible for some individual plants to pollinate their own flowers, this is not ideal because inbreeding limits them genetically. Many plants have developed some factor that promotes cross-pollination between different individuals of the same species.

Dioecious plants (those with separate male and female plants) achieve cross-pollination by their very nature. No self-pollination is possible

because each plant produces either male or female parts only.

Monoecious plants (those that produce both female and male flower parts on the same plant) avoid self-pollination by having their male or female parts mature at different times. Protandrous flowers produce pollen before the stigma is ripe and ready to receive it. The situation is reversed in the case of protogynous flowers, in which the stigma is ready to receive pollen from other flowers before its stamens ripen and produce their own. In cases where the male and female structures mature at the same time, the physical separation of the stamens and stigma can also help prevent self-pollination. Other species are genetically designed so that pollen from the same flower, or from other flowers on the same plant, cannot cause fertilization. This design – known as self-incompatibility – ensures that seed production results only from cross-pollination with a separate plant.

Right: Grasses have very small, fine and lightweight seeds that are dispersed quickly in the slightest breeze. This method of seed dispersal can carry the seeds far away from the parent plant.

Above: A common sparrow feeding on Kniphofia species aids the pollination process as it eats. Like other birds its pointed beak can reach high into tubular flowerheads to collect food.

Despite the genetic benefits of cross-pollination, however, self-pollination is the norm in some species. It may be desirable where a given genotype is particularly adapted to an environment. Another advantage is that the species does not have to depend on pollination agents to reproduce.

SEEDS AND SEED DISPERSAL

For flowering plants, seed production is the main method of reproduction. Seeds have the advantage of providing the plants with a way to spread and grow in new places, which in some cases may be at a distance from the parent. Their ability to do this is extremely important.

If seeds were not dispersed the result would be many germinating seedlings growing very close to the parent plant, leading to a crowded mass of the same species. Each of the seedlings would be in direct competition with the others, and with the parent plant, for light, space, water and nutrients. Few of the offspring (or the parent) would prosper from this arrangement.

Seeds are dispersed using a number of different strategies. The majority tend to be carried by wind, water or animals, though some plants have adopted the strategy of shooting seeds out explosively.

Wind dispersal

Seeds that depend upon wind dispersal are usually very light in weight. Orchid seeds, for example, are almost as fine as dust and easily float along in a light breeze. In addition to lightness, composite flowers such as the dandelion, *Taraxacum officinalis*, have hairy appendages on each seed that act like parachutes, carrying the seeds over long distances. In species such as the field poppy, *Papaver rhoeas*, the wind plays a part in dispersal by causing the ripe fruits to sway to and fro, shaking

Above: For plants growing near the water's edge, the water may act to transport the seed far from the parent plant.

out the seeds like pepper from a pepper pot. These seeds are often very light and small and may be carried farther away by the wind.

The small size of wind-dispersed seeds is reflected in the amount of food

reserves stored in them. Larger seeds contain greater food reserves, allowing the young seedlings more time to grow before they must begin manufacturing their own food. The longer a seedling has before it must become self-sufficient, the greater its chance of becoming successfully established. However, large seeds have the disadvantage that they are more difficult to disperse effectively by wind or explosive techniques.

Explosions

Some plants have pods that explode when ripe, shooting out the seeds. Many members of the pea family, Papilionaceae, scatter their seeds in this way. Once the seeds are ripe and the pod has dried, it bursts open and the seeds are scattered. In some of these plants, such as common gorse, *Ulex europaeus*, seed dispersal is further enhanced because the seeds possess a waxy cuticle that encourages ants to carry them around, moving them further from the parent plant. Another explosive technique is used by the

Below: In some species such as the opium poppy, Papaver somnifera, *the wind sways the ripe fruits, shaking out the seeds like pepper from a pepper pot. The wind then carries the seeds away from the parent plant.*

Below: The Mediterranean squirting cucumber, Ecballium elaterium, *has a fleshy, almost liquid fruit that, when ripe, squirts its jelly-like contents – along with the seeds – some distance from the plant.*

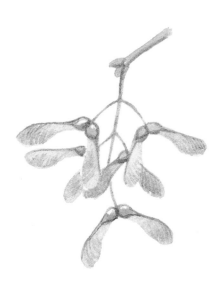

Above: Seeds of the sycamore tree are held in "keys", which float on the wind and disperse the contents far from the parent plant.

Mediterranean squirting cucumber, *Ecballium elaterium*: it has a fleshy, almost liquid, fruit that, when ripe, squirts its jelly-like contents – along with the seeds – some distance from the plant.

Water dispersal

The fruit and seeds of many aquatic or waterside plants are able to float. Water lily seeds, for example, are easily dispersed to new locations when carried by moving water, and coconuts can travel huge distances across seas and oceans, which is why coconut palms grow on so many Pacific islands – the original nuts were carried there on ocean currents from the mainland. Mangroves, which are the dominant vegetation of coastal marshes in the tropics, are another example of plants that disperse their seeds by water.

Animal dispersal

The production of a nutritious, fleshy fruit that animals like to eat is another strategy that many plants have adopted. An animal eating the fruit digests only the fleshy outer part. The well-protected seeds – the stones or pips in the fruit – pass through the animal's digestive system and are excreted in droppings that provide a

rich growing medium to get the plant started. The seeds are often deposited a long way from the parent plant by this means.

Many types of mistletoe have sticky fruits that are attractive to birds. The sticky berries create equally sticky droppings that the bird needs to "rub off" on the branches of trees. The seeds are deposited, with the droppings, on the bark to grow into new mistletoe plants.

A few plants, such as common burdock, Arctium pubens, produce seeds with hooks that catch on the fur of animals and are carried away. The animal eventually removes the burrs through grooming or moulting, and the seeds are then deposited on the ground.

Fire

Some plants living in fire-prone areas have evolved traits that allow them to use this to their advantage when reproducing or regenerating. For most of these species, the intensity of the fire is crucial to seed dispersal: it must be hot, but not so hot that it cooks the seed. In addition, fires should not occur too frequently, as the plant must have time to grow and mature so that new seed can be produced.

Many fire-tolerant species have cones that open only after a fire. Plants using this strategy are described as serotinous. Many plants that grow in

Above: Squirrels are well-known collectors of nuts, which they bury in the ground and may never return to collect.

the Australian bush or in the fynbos (the natural vegetation of South Africa's southern Cape region) are very reliant on fire. In many cases the heat triggers seed dispersal but it is the chemical constituents of the smoke that initiate seed germination.

Below: While fire decimates crops and forces wildlife out of the immediate vicinity, the heat generated by fire can trigger germination in some plant species.

HERBACEOUS PLANTS

Looking at plants in the wild, it quickly becomes apparent that there are two basic types. Those that have permanent woody stems, whose shoots do not die back, are generally referred to as trees and shrubs. The remainder lack permanent stems and are often described as herbaceous plants, or herbs.

Herbaceous plants are those that die to the ground each year and produce new stems in the following growing season. The word is used in a broader sense, however, to describe any plant with soft, non-woody tissues, whether it is an annual, perennial or bulb.

To understand how these plants live

Below: Grasslands are an ideal habitat for many herbaceous plants and provide a home for a rich diversity of species.

and grow, we can begin by looking at a seedling. In all seedlings and small plants it is the water content of the cells in the leaves and stems that holds the plants erect. All young plants are similar in this respect but as they grow, woody plants begin to build up the strengthening layers of their characteristic structure. Non-woody plants, on the other hand, always retain soft stems.

Above: The water hyacinth, Eichhornia crassipes, *is a non-woody plant that has become adapted to an aquatic lifestyle.*

Stem structure

Soft stems remain upright because their cells have rigid walls, and water in the cells helps retain their shape. This has the obvious disadvantage that during a dry period water can be drawn out of the cells; the cells become limp and the plant droops or wilts. Many species have stems with a soft inner part – commonly called the pith – that is used to store food. Others, however, have hollow cylindrical stems. In these, the vascular bundles (the veins that transport water, nutrients and sugars around the plant) are arranged near the outside of the stem. This cylindrical formation gives the stem a much greater strength than a solid structure of the same weight.

The relatively short lifespan of non-woody plants (compared with that of many woody plants) and the lack of a strong, rigid structure generally limit the height to which they can grow. Despite this, plants such as the giant hogweed, *Heracleum mantegazzianum*, can easily reach heights of 3–4m/10–13ft – larger than many shrubs. Such giants are rare, however, and most herbaceous plants are no more than 1–2m/3–6½ft in height.

Survival strategies

Non-woody plants usually produce completely new stems each year, because cold or other adverse weather (such as drought) causes the stems to die back to the ground. The climate in which the plant grows greatly affects the survival strategy it adopts. Some species survive periods of cold by forming underground bulbs or tubers for food storage, while others – the annuals – complete their life cycles within one growing season, after which the whole plant dies.

Herbaceous plants are generally divided into those with broad leaves (called forbs) and grass-like plants with very narrow leaves (called graminoids). Some species have become herbaceous vines, which climb on other plants. Epiphytes have gone one step further: they germinate and live their whole life on other plants, never coming in contact with the soil. Many orchids and bromeliads are epiphytes. Other species have adapted to life largely submerged in water, becoming aquatic plants. Many of these are rooted in the sediment at the bottom of the water, but a few have adapted to be completely free floating.

Below: Open woodland and forest clearings are often rich in herbaceous plants that enjoy the shelter and light shady conditions.

Right: Bulbs such as this petticoat daffodil, Narcissus bulbocodium, *flower in spring in alpine pasture before dying down to avoid the hot dry summer.*

A few species have adapted to use the efforts of other plants to their own ends. Some are semi-parasites – green plants that grow attached to other living, green plants. These unusual plants still photosynthesize but also supplement their nutrients by "stealing" them directly from their unfortunate host plants. A few species, however, are wholly parasitic – totally dependent upon their host for nutrition. They do not possess any chlorophyll and are therefore classed as "non-green" plants. Many remain hidden, either inside the host plant or underground, appearing to the outside world only when they produce flowers.

Subshrubs

Some plants, while they are woody in nature, resemble non-woody plants because of their small size coupled with their ability to shoot strongly from ground level or from below ground. They are known as "subshrubs", a term borrowed from horticulture, where it is used to describe any plant that is treated as a herb in respect of its cultivation. In terms of wild plants it is used rarely to describe low-growing, woody or herbaceous evergreen perennials whose shoots die back periodically.

Small plants

The world's smallest plant species is water meal, *Wolffia globosa*, a floating aquatic herb which, when mature, is not much larger than the full stop at the end of this sentence. Despite its small size, it is a flowering plant. The flowers occur only rarely and would be hard to see without the aid of a microscope. It mainly reproduces vegetatively and quickly forms a large floating colony on the surface of slow-flowing or still water.

WOODY PLANTS

Any vascular plant with a perennial woody stem that supports continued growth above ground from year to year is described as a woody plant. A true woody stem, however, contains wood, which is mainly composed of structured cellulose and lignin.

Cellulose is the primary structural component of plants, and lignin is a chemical compound that is an integral part of the cell walls. Most of the tissue in the woody stem is non-living, and although it is capable of transporting water it is simply the remains of cells that have died. This is because most woody plants form new layers of tissue each year over the layer of the preceding year. They thus increase their stem diameter from year to year and, as each new layer forms, the underlying one dies. So big woody plants are merely a thin living skin stretched over a largely lifeless framework of branches. In effect, as a woody plant grows, the proportion of living material compared to the non-living parts steadily decreases.

Bamboos appear to be woody plants, and indeed do have permanent woody stems above the ground, but are more akin to the grasses, to which they are closely related, than to the commoner woody species. Essentially, they grow a dense stand of individual

Below: Bamboos are the only examples of the grass family to have evolved permanent stems above ground.

Above: All woody plants can be defined by their permanent, often long-lived growth.

stems that emerge from underground stems called rhizomes. In many ways their biology is more like that of non-woody plants, despite their appearance.

Pros and cons of woody stems

There are more than 80,000 species of tree on earth and a considerably higher number of shrubby species. Although the exact number is not known, it is obvious even to a novice plant spotter that woody plants are an extremely successful group. This is because they are bigger than other plants, so they are able to gather more light and therefore produce more food. In areas where inclement weather induces plants to enter a seasonal dormant period, woody plants have the advantage of a head start when growth restarts. They do not have to compete with other emerging plants and can start producing a food from the moment they recommence growth.

Despite their obvious success, however, woody plants have not managed to dominate the entire

land surface. Only the largest trees are fully immune to the effects of large plant-eating mammals, and in some areas, such as the tundra, weather patterns are so extreme that only low-growing woody plants can survive, and they must compete with the surrounding herbage.

Support strategies

As well as trees and large shrubs, there are woody species that exploit other woody plants around them. Lianas, for instance, germinate on the ground and maintain soil contact, but use another plant for support. Many common climbers or vines are lianas.

Somewhat more unusual are the hemi-epiphytes, which also use other plants for support, at least during part of their life: some species germinate on other plants and then establish soil contact, while others germinate on the ground but later lose contact with the soil. The strangler figs, *Ficus* species, are interesting examples: they begin life as epiphytes,

Below: Woody plants include the largest living plant species, the giant redwood Sequoiadendron giganteum, *among their ranks.*

Above: The permanent stems of woody plants are prone to disease, such as this canker, and older specimens contain much deadwood.

Above: Mistletoe is a shrubby plant that has adapted to be partially parasitic on other, larger woody plants such as trees.

Above: Cacti are highly specialized plants that are descended from woody ancestry and have highly specialized permanent stems.

growing on other trees, unlike other tree seedlings that have to start their struggle for survival on the forest floor. The young strangler fig grows slowly at first, as little water or food is available to it, but its leathery leaves reduce water loss. It then puts out long, cable-like roots that descend the trunk of the host tree and root into the soil at its foot. Now readily able to absorb nutrients and water, the young fig tree flourishes. The thin roots thicken and interlace tightly around the supporting tree trunk. The

Below: Evergreen shrubs, such as this Rhododendron ponticum, produce food all year round and may form dense understory in deciduous woodland.

expanding leafy crown of the strangler shades the crown of the support tree and its roots start to strangle its host. The host tree eventually dies and slowly rots away, leaving a totally independent strangler fig, which may live for several hundred years.

Other woody plants, such as the mistletoe, "plug" themselves into a branch of a living tree and harvest nutrients directly from it. Apart from a free supply of food and water they gain the added advantage of being high above competing plants and trees, so that they receive enough light to photosynthesize. Mistletoe is a partial parasite that retains its woody stems and green leaves.

The largest plants

The identity of the world's largest plant is debatable, not only because woody plants are only partly living tissue, but also because it has still not been fully researched. In practice, it is extremely difficult to measure how much of a tree is actually living tissue, although the usual candidate is the giant redwood, *Sequoiadendron giganteum*. The banyan tree, *Ficus benghalensi*s, can easily cover an area of 2 hectares/5 acres, and the related *Ficus religiosa* can allegedly cover even more. Whether any of these species are really the largest is a moot point, but it is certain that the title of largest flowering plant will always be held by a woody species.

The oldest plants

Among the oldest plants on Earth are the bristlecone pines, *Pinus longaeva*. Some individuals are known to be more than 4,000 years old and others are estimated to be 5,000 years old. Some creosote plants, *Larrea divaricata* ssp. *tridentata*, are even older. The creosote plant sends up woody stems directly from ground level, so that all the stems in a dense stand are clones of the original plant. An ancient stand in California's Mojave Desert, known as the King's Clone, is estimated to be 11,700 years old, although the individual stems live for much shorter periods.

ECOLOGY AND HABITATS

The study of the ways in which plants, animals and their environment interact with one another is known as ecology. All evolutionary change takes place as a direct response to the ecological pressures that affect the plants and animals in a particular habitat.

Ecology is a scientific discipline that contributes greatly to our understanding of all living things and of evolution. The pressures that affect plants and animals in any given habitat may be a result of direct interaction between species – for example, plants may be grazed by animals – or they may be the result of changes in the wider environment, such as the changing seasons or the effect of flooding. Sometimes the effects of these interactions may be noticed across many habitats, on a regional or even global scale.

Interaction

In order to understand the complexities of even relatively small habitats, three basic principles must be remembered. First, living things do not exist as isolated individuals or groups of individuals. They are part of a continuum of life that stretches across the entire surface of the earth. Second, all organisms interact with other

Below: Plants such as the California poppy, Eschscholzia californica, *are vulnerable to habitat loss.*

members of their own species, with other species, and with their physical and chemical environments. Third, all organisms have an effect on each other and their surroundings, and as they interact with both they may actually change them over time: for example, trees gradually modify the soil they grow in by constantly dropping dead leaves that decompose and are incorporated into it.

Plant groups

The plants within an environment are grouped together in a number of ways.
• A "species" is a natural group of individuals that interbreed, or have the potential to do so, and will not normally interbreed with other related groups.
• A "population" describes all the individuals of a given species in a defined area, such as all the dandelions in an area of grassland.
• A "community" refers to the total grouping of all the different populations that occur together in a particular area.
• An "ecosystem" is the community, or

Above: Grazing animals may change or even destroy habitats where densities of animals become too high.

series of communities, together with the surrounding environment. It includes the physical and chemical environment, such as the rocks, water and air.

In an ecosystem, all the organisms composing the populations and communities require energy for survival. In the case of the plants, that energy comes from the sun: plants use sunlight for photosynthesis, which

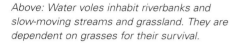

Above: Water voles inhabit riverbanks and slow-moving streams and grassland. They are dependent on grasses for their survival.

converts the light energy into basic sugars, which the plant uses as its food and stores in the form of sugars, starches and other plant material. Any animals in the ecosystem derive their energy from this store, either by eating the plants or by eating other animals that feed on the plants.

Habitats

The location where a particular species is normally found is its "habitat". A single ecosystem may contain many different habitats in which organisms can live. Salt marsh ecosystems, for example, include areas that are flooded twice daily by tides as well as areas that are inundated only by the highest tides of the month or the year. Different plants inhabit each of these areas, though there may be some overlap, but they are all considered inhabitants of the same ecosystem. Some plants can thrive and reproduce in several different habitats, as long as each provides the appropriate combination of environmental factors: the correct amount of light, water, the necessary temperature range, nutrients, and a substrate on which to grow: sand, clay, peat, water or even another plant may be appropriate. All these factors must be within the range of the plants' tolerance. Even a common plant will disappear from a habitat if an essential environmental factor shifts

beyond its range of tolerance. For example, sun-loving plants, such as the common daisy, *Bellis perennis*, flourish in full sun but gradually disappear when surrounding trees and shrubs grow large enough to shade the area. In general, common plants tend to be those that have adapted to withstand a wide range of conditions, whereas rare species survive only where certain narrowly defined environmental conditions exist. It is precisely because of their narrow range of tolerance that some plants become rare. Their lack of habitat may be due to gradual changes

Above: An area of stacked logs creates a miniature ecosystem of insects and creatures that are dependent upon each other and the plants around for survival. Such creatures improve the ecological balance of wildlife gardens and kitchen gardens.

over thousands or even millions of years (such as climate change) that reduce suitable areas to a few relics. Increasingly, however, loss of habitat is due to the actions of humans altering the environment.

Below: Every plant population attracts its own pollinators, and each exists for the mutual benefit of the other.

CONSERVING ENDANGERED SPECIES

Many plant species are now classified as endangered, because their long-term survival is under threat. There are many reasons for this, such as the erosion of a habitat, or the extinction of a key pollinator, and in some cases it is likely that the plant was never particularly numerous.

Extinction is a normal part of evolution – without it there would be no room for new species – but scientists are becoming increasingly concerned that the current rates of extinction are far above the rate at which species can easily be replaced. Attempts are therefore being made to prevent further loss of the world's rare plants.

Collecting wild plants

Though it may be tempting to pick and press wild plants, it is worth asking yourself why you want to do this. While it is true that some collections are undertaken as part of scientific research, some plants – especially the showier ones – have been overpicked to the extent that they have become critically endangered. In the UK, for instance, the lady's slipper orchid, *Cyprepedium calceolus*, was so admired by enthusiasts and collectors that it was eventually reduced to a single wild specimen. The impact of collecting one plant may seem insignificant, but the small actions of many individual collectors can lead to extinction. It is far better simply to admire the plant growing in the wild and leave it for the enjoyment of other visitors to the site.

Introduced alien plants

Many plants have become endangered because of competition from a new arrival. When plants are taken from their native environments and introduced elsewhere, they can often become highly invasive, ultimately displacing the native plants. There are numerous instances worldwide of whole native plant communities being threatened by introduced plant species.

Right: Over collection of the edelweiss, Leontopodium alpinum, *has resulted in it needing legal protection in Europe.*

Above: Collecting seeds from cultivated plants for propagation at home is accepted gardening practise, but plants growing in the wild should be left unpicked so that the population continues to thrive and support the eco system around it.

Climate change

It is likely that climate change will have a considerable impact on most or all ecosystems in the 21st century, and that changing weather patterns will alter the natural distribution ranges of many species or communities. If no physical barriers exist, it may be possible for species or communities to migrate. Habitats such as forest or grassland, for instance, may move to higher latitudes or higher altitudes if average temperatures increase. There is nothing new about this: at the end

of the last ice age (12,000–10,000 years ago) many plant communities moved quickly north or south in response to the rapid global warming that followed.

In most cases, the real danger to habitats arises where natural or constructed barriers prevent or limit the natural movement of species or communities. Many national parks, nature reserves and protected areas are surrounded by urban or agricultural landscapes, which will prevent the migration of species beyond their current artificial boundaries.

Protected areas

Every country in the world has defined areas that are managed for the conservation of animals, plants and other natural and cultural features. Only conservation *in situ* allows the natural processes of evolution to operate on whole plant and animal communities. It permits every link in the web of life, including invertebrates, soil microbes and mycorrhiza (fungi associated with plant roots), to function and interact fully within the

Above: Bluebells have become an endangered species in the United Kingdom because of over-picking. Extinction by methods of this kind can be addressed through better public awareness.

ecosystem and is essential to allow the continued development of resistance to fungal and other diseases.

Botanic gardens and plant collections

Living collections of rare and endangered plants are a sad but necessary inclusion in many botanic gardens around the world. Their role is often indirect in relation to conservation; they serve rather to inform visitors of the danger of extinction that faces many threatened species. However, the expertise developed in growing these plants can be very useful when growing stocks for reintroduction to the wild and may improve our understanding of the needs of threatened plant species.

Seed banks ensure that plants that are currently threatened with extinction can be preserved. The seed is gathered by licensed collectors and, after careful drying and cleaning, is stored at sub-zero temperatures. The seed bank works out the best method to grow the seed so that, if the wild

plants do vanish, the species can be successfully re-introduced. Experiments and observations indicate that many seeds will survive for decades in cold storage.

Both seed banks and living collections are best viewed as a relatively short-term standby, allowing conservationists to maintain a reservoir of variation.

Re-introduction of wild plants

When plants have become rare, endangered or even extinct, it is occasionally possible to re-introduce them to areas or habitats where they formerly grew. This is rarely a simple matter, however. Its success depends on the removal of whatever pressure made the plant rare in the first place.

The café marron, *Ramosmania rodriguesii*, was thought to have been extinct for 40 years in its natural home of Rodrigues in the Indian Ocean. However, in 1980 a teacher sent his pupils out on an exploratory trip to find interesting and rare plants. One pupil unearthed a small shrub half-eaten by goats and, when he returned to the school with a cutting, the teacher identified it as the café marron. There was little hope for its future survival as it was unable to produce seeds due to a flower mutation, but recent work at the Royal Botanic Gardens at Kew in the UK has resulted in its producing seed for the first time, and it may yet be re-introduced to the wild.

Below: Botanic gardens are artificially created environments that are professionally managed for research purposes and public enjoyment. They contain native and imported species and are often nationally important.

WILD FLOWER HABITATS

Flowering plants live on every continent and can be found from the ocean shores to the mountains. They are the most successful group of plants on earth, but there are very few that can boast the ability to live anywhere. Even the most widespread species have their limits and, ultimately, their preferred habitats.

Wetlands

All plants need water to live, but many species are likely to suffer and die if they get too much. If there is excessive water in the soil it forces the air out, ultimately suffocating the roots. Some plants, however, are specially adapted to living in wetlands.

Wetland plants grow in seasonally waterlogged or permanently wet conditions. There are many types of wetlands, including swamps, bogs, salt marshes, estuaries, flood plains, lakeshores and riversides. Wetlands occasionally support trees: these areas, known as wet woodland or swamp forests, are filled with rare species that tolerate wet, shady conditions.

Wetlands are rich in flowers, demonstrating that where land and

Below: A British hedgerow represents a complete ecosystem, mirroring a natural woodland edge.

water meet a rich habitat usually results. Until recently huge areas of wetland were being drained and turned into grassland or filled for development. While this continues apace in some places, wetlands are gaining a new stature in the 21st century. Many are now highly valued as natural sponges, in which water is retained on the land surface instead of flowing quickly to the sea, causing erosion and flooding as it goes.

Woodlands

Forest and woodland are extremely important habitats for many types of flowering plants, not least trees. Tree cover was once the natural vegetation over much of the Earth's surface and great forests stretched across vast tracts of every continent except Antarctica. Over the last 10,000 years

human activity has removed considerable amounts of this natural cover, particularly in Eurasia, and over the last century the trend has become a global one.

Despite the loss of forest, many areas remain and are very important havens for forest-dwelling flowers. Such flowers need to cope with low light levels for much (or even all) of the year, but trees provide a rich growing medium, through their decomposing fallen leaves, and may also provide homes for flowering climbers and epiphytes.

Exposed habitats

Where tree cover is not the dominant vegetation – whether due to human intervention or through natural

1 Chaplock	19 Hawthorn
2 Grasses	20 Long-tailed tit
3 Buttercup	21 Orange tip
4 Red clover	22 Early purple
5 Bugle	orchid
6 Chaffinch	23 Tufted vetch
7 Bramble	24 White stitchwort
8 White-tailed	25 Honeysuckle
bumblebee	26 Red campion
9 Carrion crows	27 Brimstone
10 Nettles	28 Wren
11 Dandelion	29 Field rose
12 Germander	30 Beech
13 Bluebell	31 Robin
14 Lesser celandine	32 Cow parsley
15 Garlic mustard	33 Dog violet
16 Bullfinch	34 Hoverfly
17 Kestrel	35 Primrose
18 Blackthorn	

Above: Flowers and all kinds of flora can survive in many seemingly inhospitable places.

changes – conditions are much more favourable to those species that need a lot of light. Exposed areas are mainly either grassland or scrubland and many support a truly dazzling array of wild flowers.

In temperate zones, open spaces are among the most diverse wild flower habitats to be encountered. Even open areas

that are the result of human intervention, such as traditional hay meadows, are capable of supporting many flowering species. These rich habitats have become increasingly rare over the last 100 years, due mainly to agricultural improvement programmes, making those that remain precious.

Life in the extreme

In challenging locations from frozen mountain peaks to the hottest deserts, flowering plants have learned to eke out a living. Habitats of this kind are often referred to as fragile, and while the idea of a fragile desert or mountaintop may seem strange, it is entirely accurate. Extreme survival specialists are finely tuned to make the best of scarce resources. If the conditions change even

slightly, plants do not always possess the right adaptations and may face extinction. Alpine plants, for instance, are much beloved by gardeners, but need specialist care, and treatment that mimics, as closely as possible, the conditions they enjoy in the wild, if they are to survive in cultivation.

SCRUBLAND AND DESERT

Much of the Earth's surface is characterized by land that is dry for much of the year. The plants that live in dry areas are specifically adapted to deal with the harsh extremes of these environments and many have become highly distinctive in appearance.

Mediterranean scrubland

Regions described as Mediterranean scrubland tend to have hot, dry summers followed by cool, moist winters. These conditions occur in the middle latitudes near continental west coasts: the Mediterranean itself, south central and south-western Australia, the fynbos of southern Africa, the Chilean matorral, and the chaparral of California. Most rainfall occurs from late autumn to early spring, and for many plants this is the prime growing and flowering season.

Although rare, this habitat features an extraordinary diversity of uniquely adapted plants – around 20 per cent of the Earth's plant species live in these regions. Most plants

that grow in these areas are fire-adapted, and actually depend on this disturbance for their survival.

Deserts

While they occur on every continent, deserts vary greatly in the amount of annual rainfall they receive and their average temperature. In general, evaporation exceeds rainfall. Many deserts, such as the Sahara, are hot all year round, but others, such as the Gobi Desert, become cold in winter.

Temperature extremes are a characteristic of most deserts. Searing daytime heat gives way to cold nights. Not surprisingly, the diversity of climatic conditions – though harsh – supports a rich array of habitats. Many are ephemeral in nature and often reflect the scarcity and

Above: Where vegetation is present, woody-stemmed shrubs and plants tend to be characteristic of desert regions.

seasonality of available water. Despite their harsh conditions, many deserts have extraordinarily rich floras that in some cases feature high numbers of species that are endemic.

Below: Australian mallee grows at the edge of desert regions and contains plants that are both fire- and drought-resistant.

1 Lehmann's mallee
2 *Melaleuca spicigera*
3 Clustered everlasting
4 Black kangaroo paw
5 Spiny cream spider flower
6 Cough bush
7 Azure daisy bush
8 Red kangaroo paw
9 Cactus pea
10 Hakea wattle

CONIFEROUS WOODLAND

Among the most ancient of flowering plants, conifers once dominated the whole of the Earth's surface. In modern times, however, they have become more restricted as broad-leaved flowering plants have become the dominant group.

Boreal forest

Also known as taiga or northern coniferous forest, boreal forest is located south of tundra and north of temperate deciduous forests or grass-lands. Vast tracts of this forest span northern North America, Europe and Asia. Boreal forests cover around 17 per cent of the Earth's surface. They are characterized by a cold, harsh climate, low rainfall or snowfall and a short growing season. They may be open woodlands with widely spaced trees or dense forests whose floor is in shade. The dominant ground cover is mosses and lichens, with a few specialized flowering plants.

Above: Coniferous woodland has a simple structure, a canopy layer and an understorey.

Tropical coniferous forest

Found predominantly in North and Central America, in tropical regions that experience low levels of rain and moderate variability in temperature, these forests feature a thick, closed canopy, which blocks light to the floor and allows little to grow beneath. The ground is covered with fungi and ferns and is usually relatively poor in flowering plants.

Temperate rainforest

In temperate regions, evergreen forests are found in areas with warm summers and cool winters. Conifers dominate some, while others are characterized by broadleaved evergreen trees.

Temperate evergreen forests are common in the coastal areas of regions that have mild winters and heavy rainfall, or in mountain areas. Temperate conifer forests sustain the highest levels of plant material in any land habitat and are notable for trees that often reach massive proportions.

Below: A conifer forest of north-western North America contains a wide variety of flowering plants.

1 Dogwood
2 Fireweed
3 Meadow goldenrod
4 Tiger lily
5 Calypso
6 Bunchberry
7 Yellow fawn lilies
8 Wood nymph
9 Rocky mountain lilies
10 Spring beauty
11 Dwarf waterleaf

HEDGEROWS

Many agricultural landscapes are defined by hedgerows, which are important habitats for many plants.
A hedgerow is formed of a row of intermeshing shrubs and bushes and sometimes trees that form a
boundary to keep in live stock, and are home to a diverse range of creatures.

Though a product of human activity, not all hedgerows were planted: they are sometimes relics of former habitats and may even be the oldest feature in a landscape, providing important evidence of its historic development. In the UK, for instance, the oldest hedges are probably the remains of the ancient woodland that used to cover most of the country. As villagers and landowners cleared the forest for agricultural purposes, they would leave the last narrow strip of woodland to mark the outer boundaries of their land.

Species diversity

At the heart of an ancient hedgerow is a dense shrub layer; at intervals along it trees form a broken canopy. At ground level a rich layer of herbs grows along the base of the hedge, at

Above: Hedgrows are the corridors in which small animals, such as mice, thrive, and are home to a myriad of insects and birds.

the field edge. The older the hedgerow, the greater diversity of animal and plant life it will support. The easiest way to age a hedge is to mark out a 30m/33yd stretch then count the number of different species of trees and shrubs it contains. It is reckoned to take about a hundred years for each woody plant to establish itself, so for each different species you find you can add a century to the age of the hedge. Hedgerows are very important habitats as they combine the characteristics of two other habitats – woodlands and

Below: Hedgerows combine attributes of merging habitats.

1 Dog rose
2 Honeysuckle
3 Lesser celandine
4 Red campion
5 Foxglove
6 Blackthorn

open fields. They are "corridors" for wildlife, allowing species to disperse and move from one habitat area to another. While it is difficult for most plants to spread across open fields, they can "travel" along the base of a hedge, which is often their only realistic refuge.

Below: Hedgerows are safe places in which birds can nest. The presence of eggs suggests a healthy hedgerow.

Vanishing hedgerows

The agricultural policies of recent decades have led to concern about the rate at which hedgerows are disappearing. Between 1984 and 1993, the length of managed hedgerows in the UK alone decreased by nearly a third. Hedgerow loss occurs not only when hedges are deliberately removed to make larger fields, but also when they are left to become derelict: if they are not regularly cut and managed, they grow into open lines of bushes and trees.

Pesticide or fertilizer damage can be a particular problem on intensively managed farmland, where weedkillers have often been applied to hedge bottoms to eliminate weeds. This has proved to be a very damaging practice for the natural wildflower population of hedgerows. Almost as damaging is fertilizer "drift" (unintentional overspill) into the hedge base, as it promotes the growth of certain plant species at the expense of others. Often, the species that are favoured are of little conservation value. As well as losing valuable flowers the animals that live in this environment perish.

Above: Hedgerows are often rich in species that have been driven from much of the surrounding landscape.

Above: Mice thrive in hedgerows that are maintained organically. They are part of the chain of life that helps to disperse seeds to another area of land.

BROAD-LEAVED FOREST

Many types of forest can be classified as broad-leaved. The principal types are temperate lowland forests, tropical rainforests and cloud forests, and tropical and sub-tropical dry forests. All of these typically have large, broad-leaved trees as their dominant vegetation.

There is considerable variation between forests of different types and in different locations in respect of the wildflowers they contain.

Temperate deciduous forest

The forests that tend to grow in cool, rainy areas are characterized by trees that lose their leaves in the autumn, in preparation for the cold, dark winter. By shedding its leaves, a tree conserves resources and avoids the hardship of maintaining a large mass of foliage through the winter months. Before falling, the leaves often turn brilliant colours, ranging from red to orange to yellow to brown. Once on the forest floor they decompose and provide a wonderfully rich soil.

Many low-growing plants that live in these areas commonly take advantage of the winter and early spring periods when the trees are bare. During this time the absence of shade allows them to complete their life cycle in a few months while (for them at least) light levels are highest. In late spring, when the trees have regrown their leaves, the forest floor is once again in deep shade. The seed of some species waits in the soil until trees fall, or are felled, before it germinates and grows in the resulting clearing. These plants may make a dense, showy stand for a few years before the forest

canopy, often far above the ground, closes once more and shades them out.

Temperate deciduous forests are found around the globe in the middle latitudes: in the northern hemisphere they grow in North America, Europe and eastern Asia, and in the southern hemisphere there are smaller areas, in South America, southern Africa, Australia and New Zealand. They have four distinct seasons – spring, summer, autumn and winter – and the growing season for trees in temperate forests lasts about six months.

Tropical rainforest

Very dense, warm and wet, rainforests are located in the tropics – a wide band around the equator, mostly in the area between the Tropic of Cancer (23.5° N) and the Tropic of Capricorn (23.5° S). They grow in South America, West Africa, Australia, southern India and South-east Asia.

A fairly warm, consistent temperature, coupled with a high level of rainfall, characterizes tropical rainforests. They are dominated by semi-evergreen and evergreen tree species. These number in the thousands and contribute to the highest levels of species diversity of any major terrestrial habitat type. Overall, rainforests are home to more species than any other forest habitat.

Dry forest

Tropical and sub-tropical dry forests are found in Central and South America, Africa and Madagascar, India, Indochina, New Caledonia and the Caribbean. Though they occur in climates that are warm all year round and may receive heavy rain for part of the year, they also have long dry seasons that last several months. Deciduous trees are the dominant vegetation in these forests.

Below and right: In the Northern Hemisphere, bluebells take advantage of the extra light in spring, when trees are bare, in order to grow and flower. They finish flowering just as the tree canopy above starts to fill in.

1 Bluebells

GRASSLAND

Windy and partly dry, grassland generally lacks woody vegetation, and the dominant plant type is, of course, grasses. Almost one quarter of the Earth's land surface is grassland, and in many areas grassland is the major habitat separating forests from deserts.

Grasslands, also known as savanna, pampas, campo, plain, steppe, prairie and veldt, can be divided into two types – temperate and tropical.

Temperate grassland

Located north of the Tropic of Cancer and south of the Tropic of Capricorn, temperate grasslands are common throughout these ranges. They experience a range of seasonal climatic variations typified by hot summers and cold winters. The combination of open, windy sites and dense stands of grasses mean that the evaporation rate is high, so little of the rain that falls reaches the rich soil.

The extraordinary floral communities of the Eurasian steppes and the North American plains have been largely destroyed due to the conversion of these lands to agriculture. In surviving areas of North American tall-grass prairie, as many as 300 different plant species may grow in 1 hectare/2.5 acres.

Tropical grassland

The annual temperature regime in tropical grassland is quite different to that of temperate grassland: in tropical regions it is hot all year, with wet seasons that bring torrential rains interspersed with drier seasons. Tropical grasslands are located between the Tropic of Cancer and the Tropic of Capricorn and are sometimes collectively called savannas. Many savannas do have scattered trees, and often occur between grassland and forest. They are predominantly located in the dry tropics and the subtropics, often bordering a rainforest. The plant diversity of these regions is typically lower than that of other tropical habitats and of temperate grassland.

Montane grassland

At high elevations around the world montane grasslands occur. They are found in tropical, subtropical and temperate regions, and the plants they contain often display striking adaptations to cool, wet conditions and intense sunlight, including features such as rosette structures or waxy surfaces on their leaves or stems. In the tropics these habitats are highly distinctive: examples include the heathlands and moorlands of Mount Kilimanjaro and Mount Kenya in East Africa, Mount Kinabalu in Borneo, and the Central Range of New Guinea, all of which support ranges of endemic plants.

Flooded grassland

Common to four of the continents, flooded grassland (as the name suggests) is a large expanse or complex of grassland flooded by either rain or river, usually as part of a seasonal cycle. These areas support numerous plants adapted to wet conditions. The Florida Everglades, for example, which contain the world's largest rain-fed flooded grassland, are home to some 11,000 species of flowering plants.

Below: Characteristic plants of montane grasslands display features such as rosette structures, waxy leaf or stem surfaces.

1 Iris
2 Feverfew
3 Anemone
4 Yellow asphodel

FIELDS

Farmland, fields or paddocks are essentially an environment constructed by humans, who have altered the natural landscape for the purposes of agriculture. The general term "pasture" describes grassland, rough grazing land and traditionally managed hay meadows.

Rough pasture

There are two types of pasture – permanent and rough. Permanent pasture is closed in, fertilized and sown with commercial grass species. It is often treated with herbicides that allow only a few species of grass to grow, so that it does not support a wide range of wildlife species. Rough pasture is usually much older and is typically land that is very difficult to plough so is left undisturbed.

Pasturelands owe their existence to farm livestock, and are very sensitive habitats that can easily be over- or undergrazed. They generally contain a single early stage of native vegetation, which is prevented from developing further by grazing; if the animals are removed, shrubs quickly establish and woodland develops soon afterwards. This is because many livestock animals graze very close to the ground and, while this does not damage grasses (which regrow from just above their roots), many taller plants cannot tolerate it. Grazing animals also

Above: California poppies and lupines form colourful swathes in North American grasslands.

remove nutrients from the environment so many traditional grassland areas are fairly infertile.

The wildflowers of pasture are species that grow low and thus avoid being eaten by animals. They may creep or form low rosettes of leaves and, although diminutive in general, they often have large, showy flowers that readily attract pollinators.

Below: Pasture that has been left undisturbed and unmanaged is full of life, some of which may be readily found only in that habitat.

Meadows

A true meadow is a field in which the grasses and other plants are allowed to grow in the summer and are then cut to make hay. The plants are cut while still green and then left in the field to dry. In many countries this has been the traditional method of providing feed for cattle during the winter. Hay meadows support a huge range of wild flowers, some of which have become extremely rare as traditional haymaking has been superceded by modern farming methods.

Crop fields

Many fields are used to grow crops other than grass, such as grains or vegetables. In these situations, weed species often find the conditions to their liking and thrive there. Many of these are annual flowers and some – such as cornflowers, *Centaurea cyanus*, or poppies, *Papaver rhoeas*, in wheat fields – are colourful additions to the agricultural landscape.

1 Poppy
2 Oxeye daisy
3 Hedge wound wart
4 Buttercup

HEATHS

Heaths are open landscapes that are usually treeless. Their vegetation consists largely of dwarf woody shrubs such as heathers. They are divided into two main types: upland heath (usually called moorland) and lowland heath.

Lowland heath

These habitats are under threat. They are restricted to the British Isles, northern Germany, southern Scandinavia and adjacent, mainly coastal, parts of western Europe, but equivalent vegetation types occur in cooler regions elsewhere in the world.

Lowland heath usually occurs where forest cover has been removed, usually as a result of human action, so to a large extent this is a habitat created by people. However, it can also occur on the drying surfaces of blanket bogs and fenland. In all cases, the soil under heathland is poor, with most of the nutrients having been leached from the topsoil by water. Heathland also occurs near the sea. Coastal heaths are more likely to be the result of natural factors such as the soil type and especially the exposure to high wind, which suppresses tree growth.

Above: Coastal heathlands are often exposed to high winds that cause a stunted growth.

Climate and soil

For lowland heath to occur, the climate must be "oceanic", with relatively high annual rainfall (60–110cm/24–43in) spread evenly throughout the year. The relative humidity remains moderately high even in the driest months. Winters are rarely very cold and summers rarely get very hot.

The continuous rain seeping into and through the soil promotes leaching (the loss of plant nutrients) and soils are poor as a result. If forest establishes in these areas it does not suffer from this nutrient loss – trees can maintain virtually all their nutrients within the living vegetation. It is possible that slow nutrient loss from a forest ecosystem will eventually lead to a patchwork of forest, scrub and heath. Under normal circumstances, either grazing or fires are necessary to prevent the re-invasion by scrub or colonizer tree species.

Plant adaptations

The term "heath" is derived from the heather plant, and heathers, *Erica* species, form a major part of the vegetation. Heathlands are mostly species-poor. All the species that are present in a given area ultimately look remarkably similar. In open and often windswept conditions all the species present will possess minute leaves with adaptations such as sunken stomata to minimize water loss through transpiration.

Below: Heathland is often species-rich despite the poor soils.

1 Oak
2 Euphorbia
3 Lavender
4 Juniper
5 Broom
6 Strawberry tree
7 Thyme
8 Rosemary

MOUNTAINS AND MOORLAND

Collectively, mountains and upland areas make up around 20 per cent of the world's landscape, and about 80 per cent of our fresh water originates in them. Upland heath, or moorland, occurs at altitudes above 300m/1,000ft in most temperate zones but may be found at much higher altitudes in the tropics.

Mountains

All mountain ranges feature rapid changes in altitude, climate, soil, and vegetation over very short distances. The temperature can change from extremely hot to below freezing in a matter of a few hours. Mountain habitats harbour some of the world's most unusual plants, and collectively they are home to a huge range of species. This diversity is due to their range of altitude, which results in distinct belts, or zones, of differing climates, soils and plantlife.

Vegetation on a mountain typically forms belts. This is because as the altitude increases the temperature steadily decreases – by about 2°C per 300m/3.5°F per 1,000ft. This, coupled with the thinning of the atmosphere, leads to unusually high levels of

Left: Mountain vegetation often forms distinct belts according to the altitude.

ultraviolet light and means that as plants grow higher on the mountainside they need special adaptations to survive. Typically as the altitude increases the plant species become increasingly distinct.

Below: Mountains are often isolated habitats and may contain a unique diversity of species.

Moorland and upland heath

The vegetation in moorland regions is similar in character to that of lowland heath, but it grows on deep layers of peaty or other organic soil. Moorland characteristically occurs below the alpine belt and (usually) above the tree line. It is typically dominated by dwarf shrubs, such as heather, over an understorey of small herbs and mosses.

Natural moorlands (those which are largely unmanaged by people) are generally diverse habitats, containing stands of vegetation at different stages of growth. Animal grazing and burning may be the only factors preventing them from developing into scrub or woodland.

1 Gladiolus
2 Lobelia wollastonii
3 Protea
4 Giant groundsel
5 Saxifrage
6 Umbellifer
7 Mosses

TUNDRA AND ALPINE HABITATS

In the areas nearest the poles, and in the high mountainous places of the world, the conditions for plant growth become extreme. These cold, often frozen, environments present plants with a real challenge that only the hardiest species can withstand.

Cold places

The predominant habitat in the outer polar regions and on mountaintops is known as tundra. Although arctic and alpine (mountain) tundra display differences, they often support plants with similar adaptations.

Tundra is a cold, treeless area, with very low temperatures, little rain or snow, a short growing season, few nutrients and low species diversity. It is the coldest habitat to support plantlife.

Arctic tundra

The frozen, windy, desert-like plains of the arctic tundra are found in the far north of Greenland, Alaska, Canada, Europe and Russia, and also in some sub-Antarctic islands. The long, dry winters of the polar regions feature months of total darkness and extreme cold, with temperatures dipping as low as -51°C/-60°F. The average annual temperature is -12– -6°C/

10–20°F. The annual precipitation is very low, usually amounting to less than 25cm/10in. Most of this falls as snow during the winter and melts at the start of the brief summer growing season. However, a layer of permafrost (frozen subsoil), usually within 1m/3ft of the surface, means that there is very little drainage, so bogs and ponds dot the surface and provide moisture for plants. The short growing season, when the sun gains enough strength to melt the ice, lasts for only 50–60 days. Ironically, the surface snow that marks the end of the growing season acts as an insulating blanket, ensuring that the plants do not freeze solid in winter.

The tundra supports communities of sedges and heaths as well as dwarf shrubs. Most of these plants are slow-growing and have a creeping habit, interweaving to form a low springy mass. This adaptation helps to avoid the icy winds and lessen the chances of being eaten by large grazing animals.

Above: Despite their harshness, tundra and alpine regions often support showy species.

Alpine tundra

Above the tree line and below the permanent snow line, alpine tundra is located high in mountains worldwide. In contrast to the arctic tundra, the soil of alpine tundra is very well drained and may become quite dry during the growing season, which lasts for about 180 days. Nighttime temperatures are usually below freezing.

Below: The tundra's short growing season often results in brief but dazzling displays of colour.

1 Cotton grass
2 Arctic poppy
3 Arctic forget-me-not
4 Cinquefoil

CLIFFS AND ROCKY SHORES

Rocky coasts and cliffs occur where the underlying rocks are relatively resistant to the constant pounding of the sea, rain and wind. They are found along coasts. Often the landscape is one of grandeur, characterized by steep cliffs, rocky outcrops and small bays with deep, usually clear, offshore waters.

Coastlines

Rocky coasts are often quite exposed and the constant exposure to salt-laden winds, coupled with a shortage of soil in which plant roots can anchor themselves, reduces the range of plants to a few specialist species.

Cliffs

Coastal cliffs, especially those in exposed locations, are often drenched in salt spray as the sea is driven on to the shore. Plants that grow above the spray line, out of reach of the waves and regular salt spray, are likely to be salt-tolerant, whereas those on the beach at the bottom of a cliff, or in rock crevices that are sometimes washed by salt spray, must be tolerant of salt to survive. Plants rarely grow near the base of cliffs that rise directly from the sea because the high wave energy prevents them from becoming established.

Above: Many coastal plants, such as thrift, flower profusely despite their small size.

The exposure and lack of soil in all but the deeper rock crevices means that the plants that live on cliffs often face a similar challenge to those found in the higher rocky areas in mountain ranges. This is why they often show similar adaptations, such as deep roots, creeping or hummocky growth habit and the ability to withstand exposure and drought.

The rocky coast may include indentations known as fjords, formed by glaciers wearing away depressions that were subsequently flooded by the rising water following the end of the last ice age, 10,000 years ago. These fjords may have salt marshes at their head and may be surrounded by steep-sided wooded slopes, creating a rich and varied habitat.

Rocky shores

Bedrock outcrops and boulders dominate rocky shores. The lower zones of the rocks are flooded and exposed daily by the tides and support only marine plants, whereas the upper zones are flooded during unusually high tides or in strong storms. In spite of being frequently washed by seawater, salt-tolerant land plants survive here by being well rooted in crevices in the lower-lying rocks.

Below: The high winds of coastal regions mean that plants growing there are often short and ground hugging.

1 Sea lavender
2 Thrift
3 Cornish heath
4 Sea aster

BEACHES AND SAND DUNES

Coastlines are often areas of extreme biological diversity. Areas where one habitat meets another always offer an array of flora and fauna, as animals and plants from both habitats merge. Beaches may seem like the exception where plants are concerned, as they often have limited vegetation.

Beaches

Generally, beaches are made up of sand, gravel, cobbles (shingle) and fragments of seashells, corals or other sea creatures. The proportions of all of these vary from beach to beach. Level areas of sand that are exposed only during low tide are called sandflats. Although an amazing variety of animals thrive in this habitat, very few flowering plants survive, mainly because of wave action and the saltiness of seawater. Those that do grow on them usually occur near the high tide line.

Sand dunes

Usually occuring immediately inland from sandy beaches, sand dunes are found in many parts of the world but are less well developed in tropical and subtropical coastal zones, due to lower wind speeds and damper sand. There

Above: The salty conditions and unstable sandy soil can be challenging for plants.

Above: The showy flowerheads of sea holly, Eringium Maritinum, are common on dunes.

are exceptions, however, such as the vast desert dune expanses of the Namib Desert in south-western Africa.

Sand is blown from the beach and initially accumulates in a characteristic steep windward face and more gently sloping leeward face. A change to dune meadow or dune heath eventually happens as grasses establish and stabilize the dune system, usually some

way inland. These dune slacks become dominated by low scrub, which rarely exceeds 90cm/3ft in height and is often much smaller. A few larger shrubby species are also capable of invading sand dunes to form scrub and can ultimately revert to woodland.

Below: Sand dunes are mobile, and may shift by several metres per year.

1 Sea rocket
2 Sea holly
3 Sea spurge
4 Sea bindweed
5 Yellow horned poppy
6 Burnet rose

RIVERSIDES AND WETLANDS

Wetlands are being lost at an alarming rate and many species that live in them are suffering. The habitats along rivers, waterholes and streams are critical landscapes: they help to maintain water quality and the shape and form of streams, as well as supporting species diversity in surrounding habitats.

Riversides

In their upper reaches, rivers are fast flowing with no vegetation in the water, although bankside vegetation is usually present. In the lower reaches, the water is calmer, and floating leaved and semi-aquatic plants can survive.

Riverside habitats are diverse. Grazed riverside pastures, flood meadows, marshes, reedbeds and riverine forest are common features beside many rivers, although the natural richness of the soil in the river flood plain has led people to cultivate and plant crops right to the edge of the

water in many regions. Rivers may also be altered, with their curves straightened and banks raised to create flood defences. All these factors mean that truly natural riverside habitats are scarce in areas of human occupation.

Wetlands

Marshes and flood meadows are low-lying wet areas that often flood on a seasonal basis. Reedbeds occur on land that is flooded for most of the year, often at the edges of lakes or in shallow lagoons, and often support a very diverse range of plants. Fens are areas where peat has been deposited over a long period and are often associated with extensive tracts of

Above: Reedbeds are often home to a rich diversity of plant and animal species.

marshes and reedbeds. They may contain large areas of open water and shallow, slow-flowing rivers, and are found on ground that is permanently, seasonally or periodically waterlogged.

Below: Rivers are often home to a rich and varied selection of plant and animal life.

1 Coral plant
2 Bromeliads
3 Vriesia
4 Flowering tree
5 Vridia
6 Bromeliad
7 Passion flower
8 Heliconia
9 Orchid
10 Strelitzia
11 Orchid
12 Rosy orchid

ESTUARIES, SWAMPS AND COASTAL MARSHES

Rivers eventually end by flowing out into the sea. As the river slows, the material that it has carried in the water is deposited, and sedimentary deltas, wetlands, lagoons, salt marshes and swamps may be formed.

River mouth habitats are usually extremely diverse and include abundant and rare species.

Deltas

A delta is formed where a river flows into a calm sea. As the river slows down it drops its sediment, which builds up over years to create a delta. Over time, the river splits into smaller channels called distributaries. Occasionally this can happen inland where a river flows into a low-lying basin. It forms an immense low-lying wetland, such as that of the Okavango Delta in Botswana, Africa.

Below: Tropical and sub-tropical marshlands are home to many beautiful plant species.

Above: Saltwater marshes are among the most productive habitats on earth.

Marshes and swamps

Salt marshes are made up of plant communities that are tolerant of being submerged for short periods by the tide. They can be "transitional zones", which merge with nearby areas of reed swamp, sand dune, shingle, freshwater wetland or woodland, and are particularly rich in a wide variety of plants. They are often brackish (less salty than the sea but saltier than the river) and may contain a mixture of riverside and coastal vegetation types.

The term "swamp" is usually applied to warm, wet areas that are teeming with both animal and plant life. They are often (but by no means always) heavily forested, with trees that are highly adapted to waterlogged ground. Some of these areas may be very extensive and include both coastal and freshwater habitat, such as are found in the Florida Everglades.

Mangroves are marine tidal forests that are generally most luxuriant around the mouths of large rivers or sheltered bays, growing in both salt and freshwater. They are found mainly in the tropics where annual rainfall is fairly high.

1 Bald cypress
2 Floating hearts
3 Scarlet ladies tresses
4 *Thalia dealbata*
5 Sawgrass
6 Palmetto
7 Water spider orchid
8 Ghost flower orchid
9 Night fragrance orchid
10 Golden club
11 Water lettuce

OPEN WATER

Flowering plants face possibly their biggest challenge in open water. Plants living in this environment must be able to survive either submerged beneath or floating on the surface of a body of water, and all are specially adapted to allow them to do this.

Obtaining sufficient oxygen is the greatest problem facing plants that live in water. The muddy sediment at the water bottom has few air spaces, and therefore barely any oxygen present.

Lakes and ponds

A lake describes any large body of fresh water, ranging from small ponds to huge bodies of water. They can be an extremely variable habitat, ranging from almost lifeless, acidic mountain tarns to lowland lakes teeming with life. Lakes are closely associated with rivers, chiefly because some lakes are the source for rivers. Both are fresh

Below: Although certain plant species have evolved to live in the water, the richest diversity occurs where land and water meet.

Above: Open water is a challenging habitat for plants to survive in.

water and share similar characteristics, and many species are common to both habitats.

A pond is a body of water shallow enough to support rooted plants, which in time may grow all the way across it.

Slow-flowing rivers and streams

When rivers flow slowly they may support aquatic plants in a similar way to lakes. Plants that grow in slow-flowing rivers will be species that are able to root into the bottom sediment, to stop them being washed away.

As the river runs more slowly it warms up, favouring plant growth, though in areas where the banks are tree-lined this can reduce plant growth in the water. Some river plants are only semi-aquatic, growing out of the water on the bank when the stream dries up, before being re-flooded during rainy seasons.

1 Great willow herb
2 Flowering rush
3 Branched bur weed
4 Water crowfoot
5 White water lilies
6 Reed sweet grass
7 Yellow flag iris
8 Marsh marigold
9 Hemlock water dropwort
10 Marsh thistle
11 Bullrush

WILD FLOWERS OF EURASIA AND AFRICA

Europe, Africa and Asia, are collectively described as the "Old World", to differentiate this region from the "New World" – the name that was given to the newly discovered Americas. The botanical diversity of the Old World regions is huge, with some of the best-known and most spectacular flowers gracing their lands. Even so, vast tracts of the continents of Europe, Asia and Africa remain largely unexplored, and botanists have only a sketchy idea of the plants that live in those areas. However, these continents are home to around two-thirds of the world's human population and the consequent pressure on natural habitats increases almost daily.

*Above from left: Wild carrot (*Daucus carrota*), greater masterwort (*Astrantia major*) and snowdrops (*Galanthus nivalis*).*

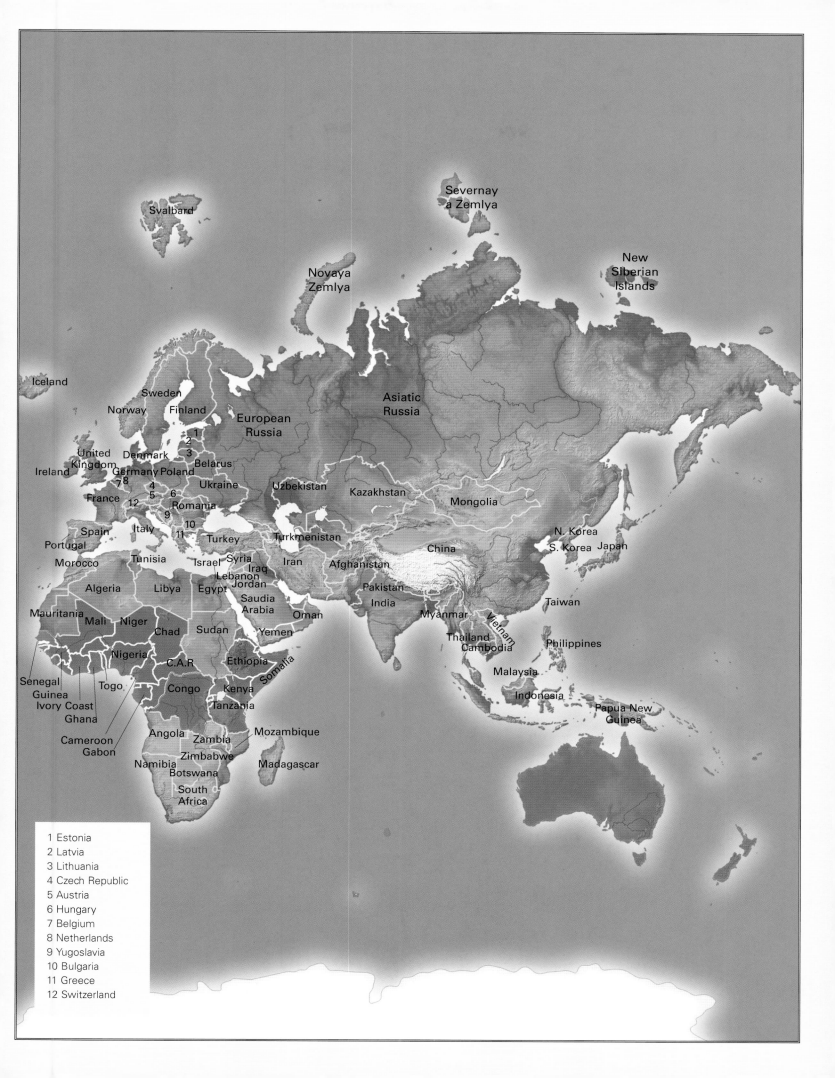

Svalbard

Severnay
a Zemlya

New
Siberian
Islands

Novaya
Zemlya

Iceland

Sweden

Norway   Finland

European
Russia   Asiatic
Russia

1
2
3

United   Denmark
Kingdom
Ireland   Belarus
                Germany Poland
                78   Ukraine   Uzbekistan   Kazakhstan   Mongolia
France   4
                    5   6
                12   Romania
                    9   N. Korea
Spain   Italy   10   S. Korea   Japan
                            11   Turkey   Turkmenistan
Portugal   China
Morocco   Tunisia   Syria   Iran
                                Israel   Iraq   Afghanistan   Taiwan
                                    Lebanon
Algeria   Libya   Egypt   Jordan   Pakistan
                                            Saudia   India   Myanmar
Mauritania   Arabia   Oman   Vietnam
            Mali   Niger   Yemen   Thailand   Philippines
                            Chad   Sudan   Cambodia
                Nigeria   Malaysia
Senegal   C.A.R   Ethiopia   Indonesia
Guinea   Somalia   Papua New
Ivory Coast   Togo   Congo   Kenya   Guinea
Ghana   Tanzania
        Cameroon   Angola   Zambia   Mozambique
        Gabon   Zimbabwe
Namibia   Botswana   Madagascar
            South
            Africa

1 Estonia
2 Latvia
3 Lithuania
4 Czech Republic
5 Austria
6 Hungary
7 Belgium
8 Netherlands
9 Yugoslavia
10 Bulgaria
11 Greece
12 Switzerland

HOW TO USE THE DIRECTORY

The directory of flowers that follow includes a diverse selection of the most beautiful wild flowers. The information below shows you how to use the directory.

The plant kingdom can be divided into two major groups: flowering plants that produce seeds (known as "higher plants") and those that do not flower, but instead produce spores (sometimes called "lower plants"). The latter group includes the mosses, liverworts, ferns and their allies. Though many of these plants are important components of habitats worldwide, it has not been possible to feature this latter group here. Among the flowering plants, the gymnosperms (conifers and cycads) have been omitted. The choice made for this book concentrates on the showy specimens that may be encountered in the wild, but also aims to illustrate the tremendous diversity of flower forms in the world.

The plants featured fall into two groups – the dicotyledonous plants are the large group, so-named because their seed has two distinct cotyledons, or embryonic leaves. The second group, the monocotyledons, contains plants that have only one seed leaf. The two groups differ evolutionarily, but both contain stunning examples of wild flower diversity.

How the directory is organized

The flowers are arranged according to their families, then genus and then species. Each family features four main plants, and up to four other flowers of note contained within a tinted box.

The introduction to each family describes common characteristics.

Each main entry discusses the primary characteristics of the plant. Wherever possible, this includes some helpful information about the type of habitat that the plant may be found in and may include other interesting facts about the species, how it interacts with wildlife and how people have used or exploited it over time. Any technical terms used in this description are supported by the glossary at the back of the book. It is followed by a detailed description to aid identification together with an accurate watercolour. A tinted box on the page describes other wild flowers of interest within the same family. Coloured maps show, at a glance, the natural distribution of the wild flowers.

Plant Family
Each wild flower belongs to a plant family. The directory of flowers is mostly arranged according to family. Each family shares a group of common characteristics, though visually the plants may seem quite different.

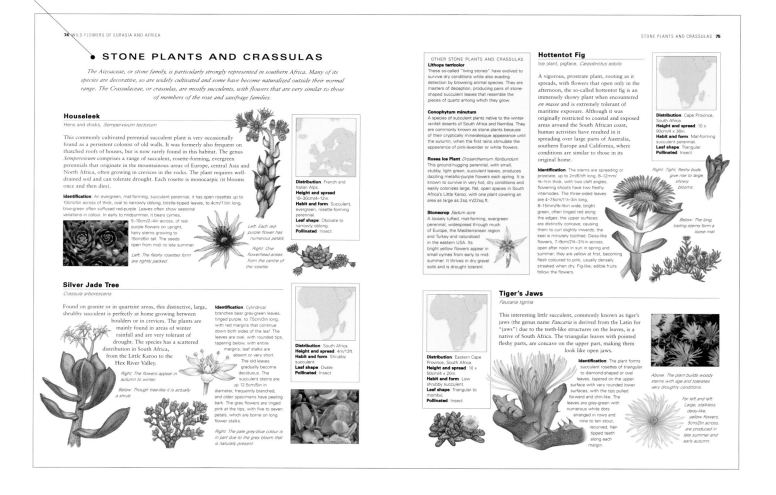

Other Common Name(s)
Some wild flowers have different common names in other regions and countries. These are listed underneath its primary common name.

Common Name
This is the most popular, non-scientific name for the wild flower entry.

Botanical Name
This is the internationally accepted botanical name for the wild flower entry. It is always in Latin.

Introduction
This provides a general introduction to the wild flower and may include information on usage, preferred conditions, and other information of general interest.

Identification
This description will enable the reader to properly identify the wild flower. It gives information on flower and leaf shape, size, colour and arrangement, and type of flower.

Tiger's Jaws
Faucaria tigrina

This interesting little succulent, commonly known as tiger's jaws (the genus name *Faucaria* is derived from the Latin for "jaws") due to the teeth-like structures on the leaves, is a native of South Africa. The triangular leaves with pointed fleshy parts, are concave on the upper part, making them look like open jaws.

Above: The plant builds woody stems with age and tolerates very droughty conditions.

Distribution: Eastern Cape Province, South Africa.
Height and spread: 10 x 50cm/4 x 20in.
Habit and form: Low shrubby succulent.
Leaf shape: Triangular to rhombic.
Pollinated: Insect.

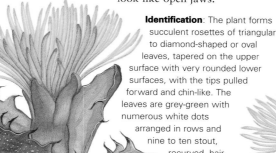

Identification: The plant forms succulent rosettes of triangular to diamond-shaped or oval leaves, tapered on the upper surface with very rounded lower surfaces, with the tips pulled forward and chin-like. The leaves are grey-green with numerous white dots arranged in rows and nine to ten stout, recurved, hair-tipped teeth along each margin.

Far left and left: Large, stalkless, daisy-like, yellow flowers, 5cm/2in across, are produced in late summer and early autumn.

Habit
The habit is the way in which a plant grows. For example, it could have an upright, sprawling or rambling habit.

Profile
The profile is a botanically accurate illustration of the plant at its time of flowering.

Plant Detail
A small detail shows an important identifying feature of the plant.

Distribution: Eastern Cape Province, South Africa.
Height and spread: 10 x 50cm/4 x 20in.
Habit and form: Low shrubby succulent.
Leaf shape: Triangular to rhombic.
Pollinated: Insect.

Map
The map shows the area of natural distribution of the featured plant. The relevant area is shaded in yellow. The natural distribution shows where in the world the plant originated. It does not mean that this is the only place where the plant now grows.

Distribution
This describes the plant's natural distribution throughout the world.

Height and spread
Describes the average dimensions the plant will grow to given optimal growing conditions.

Habit and form
Describes the plant type and shape.

Leaf shape
Describes the shape of the leaf.

Pollinated
Flora can be pollinated by many different animals and insects, as well as by the action of air.

Other family species of note
The flora featured in this tinted box are usually less well-known species of the family. They are included because they have some outstanding features worthy of note.

Species names
The name by which the plant is most commonly known is presented first, followed by the Latin name and any other common name by which the plant is known.

Entries
The information given for each entry describes the plant's main characteristics and the specific features it has that distinguish it from better known species.

OTHER STONE PLANTS AND CRASSULAS
Conophytum minutum
A species of succulent plants native to the winter-rainfall deserts of South Africa and Namibia. They are commonly known as stone plants because of their cryptically mineralesque appearance.

Stonecrop *Sedum acre*
A loosely tufted, mat-forming, evergreen perennial, widespread through much of Europe, the Mediterranean region and Turkey. Its bright yellow flowers appear in small cymes from early to mid-summer. It is drought tolerant.

BUTTERCUP FAMILY

There are around 1,800 species in the buttercup family (Ranunculaceae), and they are found mainly in the colder regions of the world. Many are well-known wild flowers, while some are more familiar as garden flowers. The group includes buttercups, anemones, delphiniums, aquilegias and clematis. Some genera are poisonous. Nearly all the buttercup family are herbaceous – clematis is the only woody genus.

Columbine

Culverwort, Granny's bonnet, *Aquilegia vulgaris*

A familiar plant because it is often seen as a garden escapee, columbine typically grows in light and medium soils and always prefers a moist situation. It is highly adaptable and can grow in full sun, the dappled shade of light woodland or in semi-shade.

Identification: A variable plant with stems branched in the upper parts to support numerous nodding, scented flowers, 2.5–4cm/1–1½in, usually blue, with spreading sepals, behind which are very short, strongly hooked spurs. It is in flower from mid-spring to midsummer. The leaves are mainly basal, dark green flushed blue, and much divided.

Far left: The distinctive flower-heads are held above the mainly basal foliage.

Right: The seedhead splits at the top to disperse seeds when rocked by breezes.

Far right: Aquilegia self seeds and spreads quickly. It has a rangy habit.

Distribution: Europe.
Height and spread: 30–70 x 50cm/12–28 x 20in.
Habit and form: Herbaceous perennial.
Leaf shape: Compound trifoliate.
Pollinated: Bee, particularly bumblebee.

Meadow Buttercup

Tall crowfoot, *Ranunculus acris*

The golden-yellow spring flowers of the European buttercup are a common sight across its natural range, but it is also widely naturalized in eastern North America, through agricultural importation. It is common in damp grassland, on roadsides and in high pastures. Unlike the equally common creeping buttercup, *R. repens*, the meadow buttercup reproduces solely by seed rather than by runners (spreading overground stems that root at the leaf joints as they touch the ground) and so forms clumps.

Identification: A tall erect herb with smooth or slightly hairy flower stalks that are held high above the foliage. The lower leaves are strongly divided into three to seven lobes. They are toothed, hairy and occasionally marked with black, with none of the lobes stalked. The showy yellow flowers are to 2cm/¾in across, with five rounded, glossy petals, which are produced in great profusion from late spring to early autumn. The sepals are pressed flat against the flower, not downturned. The fruits are rounded, with short, hooked beaks.

Above left: The small distinctive spiky round fruits swell as soon as the petals drop.

Left: The foliage is mostly basal. The flowerheads are held above this on stout, sparsely leaved stems.

Right: The distinctive sunshine-yellow flowers of the buttercup are held aloft singly, on long thin stems.

Distribution: Europe, Asia.
Height and spread: 30–90cm/1–3ft.
Habit and form: Herbaceous perennial.
Leaf shape: Palmate.
Pollinated: Insect.

Lenten Rose

Hellebore, *Helleborus orientalis*

Distribution: Eastern Europe to western Asia.
Height and spread: 45cm/18in.
Habit and form: Evergreen perennial.
Leaf shape: Palmate.
Pollinated: Insect.

This highly variable plant grows in shade or semi-shade in deciduous woodland on lower mountain slopes. There is much uncertainty as to the number of subspecies. The fact that it is such a beautiful and reliable flower of winter and early spring has resulted in its widespread cultivation, with many cultivars and hybrids being grown in gardens. As a result, it commonly occurs as a garden escapee, often way beyond its original natural distribution.

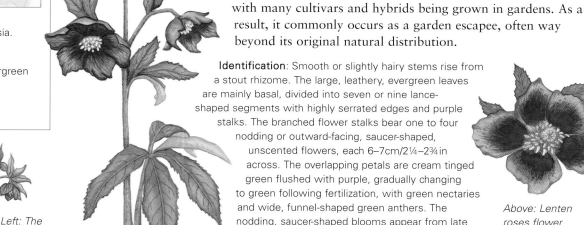

Identification: Smooth or slightly hairy stems rise from a stout rhizome. The large, leathery, evergreen leaves are mainly basal, divided into seven or nine lance-shaped segments with highly serrated edges and purple stalks. The branched flower stalks bear one to four nodding or outward-facing, saucer-shaped, unscented flowers, each 6–7cm/2¼–2¾in across. The overlapping petals are cream tinged green flushed with purple, gradually changing to green following fertilization, with green nectaries and wide, funnel-shaped green anthers. The nodding, saucer-shaped blooms appear from late winter onward, before the new foliage.

Left: The flowerheads droop.

Above: Lenten roses flower in winter.

Pheasant's Eye *Adonis annua*
This annual, also known as the flower of Adonis, grows to a height and spread of 15–30cm/6–12in. It forms clumps of green, fern-like foliage topped with deep red, anemone-like flowers in summer, chiefly on cultivated land.

Winter Aconite *Eranthis hyemalis*
This clump-forming tuberous perennial from central Europe may form quite large colonies. In late winter or early spring it produces bright yellow flowers 2–3cm/¾–1¼in across, each borne above a ruff of dissected, bright green leaves.

Monkshood
Aconitum napellus
Monkshood is a variable, erect perennial, common across much of northern and central Europe. In mid- to late summer the tall, erect flowering stems bear dense racemes of indigo-blue flowers, held above the rounded, deeply lobed, dark green leaves.

Pasque Flower *Pulsatilla vulgaris*
This clump-forming perennial is found chiefly on free-draining chalky or alkaline soils across much of Europe. The finely divided, feathery, light green leaves are very hairy when young and are topped in spring with upright or semi-pendent, silky, purple flowers.

Delphinium

Larkspur, *Delphinium elatum*

Delphiniums were so named by the ancient Greeks, who thought the shape of the flower bud resembled a dolphin. The flowers appear from early to late summer, and are mostly blue, occasionally pinkish or whitish, arranged loosely around almost the entire length of the flower spike, on robust upright stems. In Tudor England, some species in cultivation were called larkspur because the nectary looked similar to a lark's claw. The plant is encountered on roadsides and in fields, usually as a garden escapee.

Identification: The large rounded leaves are fairly deeply divided into five to seven or more coarsely toothed lobes. Each flower is 2.5–4cm/1–1½in long and up to 2.5cm/1in wide, with golden filaments in the centre and five petal-like sepals, the rear one elongated into a long, slender, curving spur; the two upper petals are united. The fruits are erect, smooth pods tipped with short beaks, open on one side.

Far right: The flower spikes are impressive, held above the foliage.

Distribution: Central and eastern Europe.
Height and spread: 90–120 x 30–60cm/3–4 x 1–2ft.
Habit and form: Herbaceous perennial.
Leaf shape: Palmate, lobed.
Pollinated: Chiefly bee.

Below: Delphinium flower spikes are made of many flowerheads.

ROSE FAMILY

The rose family (Rosaceae) includes trees, shrubs and herbs and comprises about 100 genera and 3,000 species. Most members of the family have similar flowers, commonly with five petals and numerous stamens, but their fruiting arrangements vary considerably. The rose family includes some of our best-known wild flowers and has many showy flower species in its ranks.

Sweet Briar

Eglantine, *Rosa rubiginosa*

This rose is noted for its flowers and also for the unique aroma of its leaves, which are particularly fragrant after rain. Strangely, while the leaves are so fragrant, the flowers are almost entirely without scent. It is most commonly found in open copses and old hedgerows, usually on limy soils, and will sometimes colonize chalk grassland. Because of its apple-scented foliage the sweet briar has held a cherished place in many old-fashioned gardens.

Left: Sweet briar forms an open, spreading shrub on chalky soils.

Right: Each bloom lasts a few days. New ones replace them over a period of weeks.

Identification: The sweet briar is a vigorous, arching, prickly stemmed, deciduous shrub. The leaves are dark green, with five to nine oval leaflets 2.5–4cm/1–1½in long, with a finely toothed margin. Cupped, single flowers up to 2.5cm/1in across, usually bright rose pink, appear in early to midsummer, and are followed by oval to spherical, orange-scarlet hips in late summer.

Distribution: Europe, North Africa to western Asia.
Height and spread: 2.5m/8ft.
Habit and form: Deciduous shrub.
Leaf shape: Pinnate.
Pollinated: Bee, fly, moth and butterfly.

Right: The bright red hips often last well into the winter.

Japanese Quince

Chaenomeles speciosa

The Japanese quince is noteworthy for the fact that it commences its flowering before the leaves emerge and can be in flower in late winter. It should not be confused with the related genus *Cydonia*, which is the source of the cultivated quince fruit. The plant tolerates a wide range of soils, although it prospers best in moist, well-drained soil.

Identification: A vigorous, deciduous, spreading shrub with tangled, spiny branches and oval, glossy, dark green leaves 4–9cm/1½–3½in long. In spring the branches bear clusters of two to four scarlet to crimson, five-petalled, cupped flowers, up to 4.5cm/1¾in across. The flowers are borne on bare stems and may continue well into the spring, after the foliage has emerged, followed by aromatic, green-yellow fruit.

Left: Japanese quince forms a loose sprawling shrub.

Distribution: East Asia and China, but long cultivation has obscured its natural habitat.
Height and spread: 3 x 5m/10 x 16ft.
Habit and form: Deciduous shrub.
Leaf shape: Ovate.
Pollinated: Bee.

Left: Despite the name, this quince does not yield sweet fruit like the cultivated form of Cydonia oblongata.

Blackberry

Bramble, *Rubus fruticosa*

An extremely common plant, the fast-growing bramble is found in hedgerows, woodland, meadows and on waste ground. Its blossoms and fruits (both green and ripe) may be seen on the bush at the same time, which is an unusual feature. Blackberries have a tremendous range of site and soil tolerances and can grow in full shade (deep woodland), semi-shade (light woodland), or in sun. They can tolerate drought and strong winds but not maritime exposure. Opinions differ as to whether there is one true blackberry with many aberrant forms, or many distinct types.

Distribution: European origin, but transported worldwide by humans.
Height and spread: 3m/10ft.
Habit and form: Deciduous shrub.
Leaf shape: Variable, palmate lobed or pinnate.
Pollinated: Insect, can self-pollinate.

Far left: the blackberry forms an untidy, layered and spreading thicket.

Identification: The leaves are borne on long, arching, tip-rooting stems. Brambles often form dense, impenetrable thickets along hedgerows or woodland margins. All blackberries have five-petalled, saucer-shaped, pink or white flowers, which appear in great profusion between late spring and early autumn, followed by tight clusters of black, spherical fruits.

Above: The stems carry thorns.

Left: the berries ripen from midsummer onwards.

OTHER ROSE FAMILY SPECIES

Dog Rose *Rosa canina*
The dog rose flowers in early summer. Its general habit can be quite variable. The single flowers vary widely from almost white to a very deep pink, with a delicate but refreshing fragrance. The hips are produced in autumn.

Shrubby Cinquefoil *Potentilla fruticosa*
This deciduous shrub, with a height and spread of about 120cm/4ft, is in flower from early to midsummer. The yellow flowers are dioecious and are pollinated by bees and flies.

Scarlet Geum *Geum coccineum* 'Borsii'
The moisture-loving scarlet avens originates in the Balkans and northern Turkey. A compact, clump-forming plant, it is noteworthy for its display of beautiful orange-scarlet flowers with prominent yellow stamens, on 30cm/12in stems, in late spring to late summer.

Mountain Avens *Dryas octopetala*
The small mountain avens is distinguished from all other plants of the Rosaceae by its oblong,

deeply cut leaves, which have white downy undersides, and by its large, handsome, anemone-like white flowers, which have eight petals. It blooms in midsummer.

Dropwort

Filipendula vulgaris

This tall, scented, vigorous perennial of dry soils is easily confused with meadowsweet, *F. ulmaris*, which prefers damp or seasonally waterlogged grassland. Dropwort prefers alkaline soil and cannot grow in the shade; for this reason it can sometimes be found growing at the base of an old wall. The plant is especially noted for attracting wildlife.

Identification: The abundant, fern-like dark green leaves are finely divided, toothed and hairless, with eight or more leaflets, each about 2cm/¾in long. In early and midsummer, slender, branching stems bear loose clusters, to 15cm/6in across, of white, rather sweetly scented, often red-tinged flowers. The seeds ripen from midsummer to early autumn.

Above: Each flower gives rise to tiny fruits from mid-summer onward.

Far right: The flower-heads are sweetly scented and noted for attracting wildlife.

Distribution: Northern Eurasia.
Height and spread: 75 x 40cm/30 x 16in.
Habit and form: Herbaceous perennial.
Leaf shape: Pinnate.
Pollinated: Insect, can self-pollinate.

Below: Dropwort forms a tall and attractive clump of flowering stems above the fern-like foliage.

LEGUMES

The Papilionaceae, or legumes, are so-named because of their butterfly-shaped flowers, are found in temperate and tropical areas. Ecologically, legumes are well known for fixing nitrogen in the soil through a symbiotic relationship with bacteria, which infect the roots: the plant supplies sugars for the bacteria, while the bacteria provide the biologically useful nitrogen absorbed by the plant.

Black Medick

Medicago lupulina

This common roadside plant resembles clover until the yellow flowers appear, but is distinguishable when not in flower by the extra long stalk of the middle leaflet or by the black seeds that follow flowering. It tolerates a wide range of soils but prefers well-drained ground and is common in fields and dry downland. It is one of the plants identified as shamrock and worn by the Irish to celebrate St Patrick's Day.

Identification: The leaves of this prostrate plant are three-lobed, light to mid-green with slightly serrated ends and occasional black markings. The small, pale yellow flowers emerge from the leaf axils and appear from mid-spring to late summer. They are self-fertile and are followed by small black, slightly coiled seedheads, which ripen from midsummer to early autumn.

Above: The small yellow flowers of black medick emerge from the leaf axils and often appear at the same time as the tightly coiled seedheads.

Distribution: Europe.
Height and spread: 45cm/18in.
Habit and form: Creeping herbaceous perennial.
Leaf shape: Trifoliate.
Pollinated: Insect.

Right: The small, black, slightly coiled seedheads are the feature of this plant that lead to its common name of black medick.

White Clover

Trifolium repens

This small creeping perennial is common in many grassland situations such as fields, pasture and lawns where it often forms extensive patches. It is most easily identified by the numerous erect white flowerheads that appear just above the grass. In many areas this very variable species is derived from cultivated stock rather than native plants, chiefly because of its inclusion in agricultural grass seed mixes. It is extremely common across much of Eurasia and has been spread further through agriculture. It is often mistaken for red clover, *T. pratense*, as its flowers can be tinged pink, but they lack leaves close below the flowerhead.

Identification: The prostrate stems creep extensively, rooting as they go, and white clover often forms large mats in grassy places. The leaves are trifoliate, with oval leaflets, generally about 1.5cm/⅝in across, usually with a whitish band encircling the base. The flowerheads are held on erect, leafless stalks 20–50cm/8–20in tall; they are generally white, sometimes pink-tinted, and contain up to 100 florets. The flowers persist, turning brown, to enclose the brown pods of one to four seeds.

Above: The flowers droop and turn brown once fertilized and enclose the small seedpods.

Distribution: Eurasia.
Height and spread: 20–50cm/8–20in; indefinite spread.
Habit and form: Creeping herbaceous perennial.
Leaf shape: Trifoliate.
Pollinated: Bee.

Cancer Bush

Kankerbos, balloon pea, *Sutherlandia frutescens*

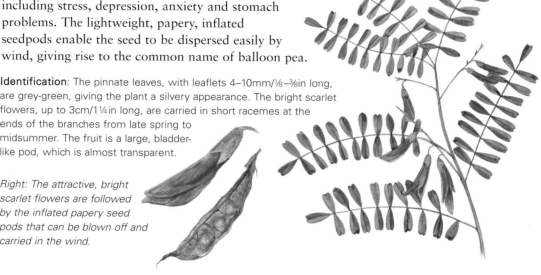

A curious South African plant, the cancer bush is an attractive, small, soft-wooded shrublet that occurs naturally throughout the dry parts of southern Africa. The leaves, which have a very bitter taste, are made into tea to alleviate a variety of ailments, including stress, depression, anxiety and stomach problems. The lightweight, papery, inflated seedpods enable the seed to be dispersed easily by wind, giving rise to the common name of balloon pea.

Distribution: South Africa.
Height and spread: 50–100cm/20–39in.
Habit and form: Shrub.
Leaf shape: Pinnate.
Pollinated: Sunbird.

Identification: The pinnate leaves, with leaflets 4–10mm/⅛–⅜in long, are grey-green, giving the plant a silvery appearance. The bright scarlet flowers, up to 3cm/1¼in long, are carried in short racemes at the ends of the branches from late spring to midsummer. The fruit is a large, bladder-like pod, which is almost transparent.

Right: The attractive, bright scarlet flowers are followed by the inflated papery seed pods that can be blown off and carried in the wind.

Hare's Foot Clover *Trifolium arvense*
This upright species grows up to 20cm/8in tall, with spreading leaves. The trefoil leaves have stipules with long spiny points. The large, mostly pink, cylindrical flowerheads are covered in soft, creamy-white hairs.

Gorse *Ulex europaeus*
An evergreen shrub from the Atlantic margin of Europe, introduced to and spreading in many parts of the world. It grows quickly on rough open ground, and has a very long flowering period, with abundant golden-yellow, scented flowers clothing the spiny branch tips.

Pride of the Cape *Bauhinia galpinii*
This medium to large clambering shrub grows in the moister areas of the southern African veldt, climbing through other trees and shrubs in dense vegetation. It has evergreen foliage and brick-red, orchid-like flowers in summer.

Everlasting Pea *Lathyrus sylvestris*
This perennial climber is widespread over most of Europe, and has stems up to 2m/6½ft long. Each leaf has one pair of leaflets and ends in a branching tendril. Large pink- and-red flowers appear on very long flower stems.

Tufted Vetch

Vicia cracca

A widespread and common climber, the tufted vetch favours grassy places, hedgerows, scrub, thickets and field boundaries. Its flower-laden stems festoon the hedgerows and long grasses of wayside places, attached by means of tendrils. It is quite variable across its range, especially in the shape and hairiness of the leaves, and is easily confused with similar species.

Identification: This scrambling perennial grows from a creeping rhizome, with angular, softly hairy stems. The pinnate leaves comprise up to 12 pairs of narrow, oblong leaflets, usually with hairy undersides, and end in a branched tendril. Flower spikes up to 4cm/1½in long, with 10–40 bluish-purple flowers in dense clusters on one side of the stalk, appear from early to late summer. They are followed by flattened, brown seedpods, 1–2.5cm/⅜–1in long, on short stalks.

Right: Each cluster has numerous purple flowers.

Far right: Tufted vetch has a scrambling habit.

Distribution: Europe.
Height and spread: Up to 2m/6½ft.
Habit and form: Climbing herbaceous perennial.
Leaf shape: Pinnate.
Pollinated: Insect.

CABBAGE FAMILY

The Brassicaceae, or cabbages, are herbs or, rarely, subshrubs. The family includes familiar food plants such as cabbage, cauliflower, broccoli, Brussels sprouts, kohlrabi and kale, which have all been derived from a single wild plant through human selection. Members of the cabbage family are found throughout temperate parts of the world, with the greatest diversity in the Mediterranean region.

Honesty

Money plant, Silver dollar, *Lunaria annua*

Honesty can often be encountered in uncultivated fields across much of Europe, although most of the plants seen in the vicinity of human habitation are probably garden escapees. The eye-catching spring blooms are rich in nectar and therefore popular with butterflies. Later in the year the plant produces masses of attractive, translucent, silvery seedpods, which are used in floral arrangements.

Identification: The plant has stiff, hairy stems and heart-shaped to pointed leaves, coarsely toothed and up to 15cm/6in long. The cross-shaped flowers appear in mid- to late spring, borne in broad, leafy racemes up to 18cm/7in long. The green seedpods are 2.5–7.5cm/1–3in across, flat and circular and firmly attached to the stems. The large seeds are strongly compressed in two rows. A thin, translucent wall is formed between the two valves of the pod during the ripening process, creating the classic "silver penny" when the seeds disperse.

Above: The flowers are pink-purple and occasionally white.

Right: The cross-shaped flowers are in loose clusters above the leaves.

Far right: The seedpods are flat and papery.

Distribution: South-east Europe and western Asia.
Height and spread: 60–90 x 30cm/24–36 x 12in.
Habit and form: Annual or biennial.
Leaf shape: Cordate-acuminate.
Pollinated: Insect.

Wallflower

Erysimum cheiri

The wallflower is very widely distributed, though it is actually a garden escapee across much of its range. It is thought to have been the result of a cross between two closely related species from Greece and the Aegean region, but this ancestry is obscure and the plant is now regarded as a species in its own right. It requires good drainage and can grow in nutritionally poor and very alkaline soil, so it is often seen colonizing old walls. It tolerates maritime exposure.

Identification: This shrubby, evergreen, short-lived perennial is in flower from mid-spring to early summer. It forms mounds of stalkless, narrow, spear-shaped, dark green leaves, to 23cm/9in long, the margins of which are smooth or have well-spaced teeth. Open, sweetly scented, bright yellow-orange flowers, up to 2.5cm/1in across, are produced in short racemes in the spring.

Distribution: Southern Europe, but widely naturalized.
Height and spread: 25–75 x 30–40cm/10–30 x 12–16in.
Habit and form: Partly woody subshrub.
Leaf shape: Lanceolate to obovate.
Pollinated: Bee and fly.

Far left: Wallflower has an open habit.

Left: The flowers are cross-shaped.

Left: The short, dense inflorescence is very attractive when it appears in the spring.

Hoary Stock

Matthiola incana

Distribution: Europe.
Height and spread: 60 x 30cm/24 x 12in.
Habit and form: Short-lived, slightly woody perennial.
Leaf shape: Lanceolate or linear lanceolate.
Pollinated: Insect, especially butterfly.

Hoary stock often resembles a wallflower growing on chalk cliffs and beside roads, where it could easily be mistaken for a garden escapee. It is the parent of the garden stocks. The flowers are highly fragrant and are said to smell of cloves. The plant prefers well-drained alkaline soils and can tolerate maritime exposure, actually prospering best in a cool, moist environment such as sea cliffs. This attractive species is noted for its tendency to attract insects, especially butterflies and bees.

Right: The long, cylindrical seed pods ripen in late summer and split along their length to disperse the seeds.

Identification: A woody-based perennial or subshrub with narrow, grey-green to white hairy leaves, which are 5–10cm/2–4in long, and are mostly entire but occasionally deeply segmented or lobed. The upright racemes of sweetly scented flowers, mostly mauve or purple but also occasionally violet, pink or white, up to 2.5cm/1in across, are borne from late spring to midsummer, and the seeds ripen in 10cm/4in pods in late summer.

Right: The plant forms an attractive hummocky mass with showy flowerheads in early summer.

OTHER CABBAGE FAMILY SPECIES

Candytuft
Iberis sempervirens
Perennial candytuft is a short, woody shrub that forms a dense mound of small, evergreen leaves, with heads of many tiny, white flowers in flat, terminal clusters at a height of 25cm/10in in spring. It is found throughout the mountains of Europe and Asia Minor.

Sweet Alyssum *Lobularia maritima*
More usually known by its previous name of *Alyssum maritinum*, this short-lived perennial from the Mediterranean forms a dense mound of small green leaves, covered from late spring in compact heads of tiny, perfumed, white or occasionally pale purple-pink flowers.

Lady's Smock *Cardamine pratensis*
Also known as cuckoo flower, this elegant plant grows in damp meadows, ditches, by ponds and streams and along woodland edges. It produces clusters of large, pale mauve to pink flowers in late spring. It is distributed across northern Eurasia and the USA.

Garlic Mustard *Alliaria petiolata*
This biennial, with dark green, kidney-shaped leaves, has a distinct garlic odour when crushed. A single flower stalk appears in spring carrying a profusion of small white flowers. Native to Europe, it is an invasive weed in many areas.

Aubretia

Wallcress, *Aubrieta deltoidea*

This carpet-forming perennial is found growing naturally among scree and on high moorland. It is very similar to rockcress, the *Arabis* species, but flowers a little later and blooms for a longer period. Its popularity in cultivation has led to its common appearance as a garden escapee, although many such plants are hybrids and the true species is generally restricted to mountains in southern Europe. The plant prefers moist but well-drained soil, although it tolerates a wide range of soil types and can survive drought and periods of hot dry weather.

Identification: An evergreen, mat-forming, slightly woody perennial, it has small, mid-green, oval leaves, hairy and slightly toothed along the margin. The blue or purple, cross-shaped, four-petalled flowers, 1.5cm/⅝in across, are produced in great profusion on small racemes, and cover the mat of leaves in late spring. The seeds ripen in early summer.

Above: The attractive, flowers appear prolifically in late spring.

Right: Aubretia forms a dense mat of stems.

Distribution: South-east Europe, Turkey.
Height and spread: 15 x 30cm/6 x 12in.
Habit and form: Slightly woody, creeping perennial.
Leaf shape: Ovate to obovate.
Pollinated: Bee.

POPPIES AND FUMITORIES

The Papaveraceae, or poppies, are herbs or rarely shrubs or trees comprising 25 genera and 200 species that usually have milky or coloured sap. The largest genus in this group is the poppies, Papaver, with about 100 species, many of which are notable for their large, showy flowers. The Fumariaceae, or fumitories, include about 19 genera, found mostly in the Northern Hemisphere.

Field Poppy

Common poppy, *Papaver rhoeas*

The field poppy is a species classically associated with heavily disturbed ground, hence its symbolic association with the battlefields of World War I. One of the reasons for this is that it has a particularly persistent seed bank. It is a common weed of cultivated land and waste places, in all but acid soils, although it is now becoming far less frequent due to modern agricultural practices.

Identification: Erect or semi-erect branching stems, sparsely bristled, exude a white sap when cut. The oblong, light green, downy leaves, to 15cm/6in long, are deeply segmented with lance-shaped lobes. Solitary, bowl-shaped, brilliant red flowers, sometimes marked black at the petal bases, to 8cm/3¼in across, are borne on short, downy stalks from early to late summer. The flowers are followed by hairless, spherical seed capsules, which release the seed from an upper ring of pores; they ripen from late summer to early autumn.

Above:
The fruiting capsule scatters tiny seeds when shaken by late summer winds.

Left: Although individual flowers are short lived, they are produced prolifically over the summer.

Distribution: Europe, widely spread through agriculture.
Height and spread: 60 x 15cm/24 x 6in.
Habit and form: Annual.
Leaf shape: Pinnatifid.
Pollinated: Insect.

Right: Field poppies form an erect, branching plant.

Himalayan Blue Poppy

Meconopsis betonicifolia

This is the classic blue poppy "discovered" by Lt Col F.M. Bailey in southern Tibet in 1913, and brought into cultivation by Frank Kingdon-Ward in 1926. It is from the rocky mountain slopes of the Himalayas and grows there in moist acidic soils, in which the blue colour develops its greatest intensity. The plant is perennial but sometimes short-lived, and though much cultivated rarely naturalizes as a garden escapee outside its natural range.

Identification: Large basal rosettes of leaves are produced in spring; they are toothed, heart-shaped or flat at the base, 15–30cm/6–12in long and light blue-green, covered with rust-coloured hairs. In early summer the flower spike grows up to 90cm/3ft. Drooping to horizontal, saucer-shaped, bright blue, sometimes purple-blue or white flowers, 7.5–10cm/3–4in across, with yellow stamens, are borne on bristly stalks up to 20cm/8in long, singly or sometimes clustered toward the top of the stem. It occasionally occurs as a pure white form var. *alba*, which is striking but is only rarely encountered outside cultivation.

Distribution: South-western China, Tibet, Burma.
Height and spread: 90 x 45cm/36 x 18in.
Habit and form: Herbaceous perennial.
Leaf shape: Oblong to ovate.
Pollinated: Insect.

Far left: The striking, erect and robust flower stems are held high over the leafy rosette.

OTHER POPPY AND FUMITORY SPECIES

Welsh Poppy *Meconopsis cambrica*
The Welsh poppy is the only species of *Meconopsis* found outside Asia and is from the woodlands and mountain rocks of western Europe. The leaves are deeply divided into irregular lobes. In spring and summer small, yellow or rich orange flowers are borne singly on slender stems.

Opium Poppy *Papaver somnifera*
The opium poppy is a robust, erect, blue-green, sparsely bristly annual that sports papery mauve, lilac or scarlet flowers that are usually purplish at the base. Although Asiatic in origin, its exact natural distribution is obscure as it has long been cultivated for its narcotic properties.

Greater Celandine *Chelidonium majus*
The greater celandine has erect slender branching stems up to 60cm/24in tall, with numerous small yellow flowers in groups of three to six in loose umbels, giving way to smooth cylindrical seedpods. It inhabits waysides and waste places in Europe, Asia and north-eastern North America.

Plume Poppy *Macleaya cordata*
The plume poppy is a handsome and vigorous perennial from Japan and China. Its stems reach 2.5m/8ft, with very large panicles of small buff white flowers that have the overall appearance of a soft creamy plume, above elegant blue-green downy leaves.

Yellow Horned Poppy
Glaucum flavum

The showy yellow horned poppy is a familiar sight along much of the coastline of Europe, North Africa and western Asia, where it occurs on shingle or gravel beaches. The golden yellow flowers of this short-lived perennial are followed in the latter part of the summer, by unusual, long, curling seedpods, which are often known as horns, hence the name. The plant exudes a yellow, foul-smelling latex when it is broken. All parts of it are poisonous.

Identification: A rosette-forming, slightly hairy plant with deeply lobed, hairless, rough, blue-green leaves, 15–30cm/6–12in long, the lobes incised or toothed. It produces branched grey stems of bright golden-yellow or orange, saucer-shaped flowers in summer; up to 5cm/2in across, they have golden anthers and a pale green pistil. The flowers are followed by the curling seedpods in late summer, which can be up to 30cm/12in long.

Distribution: Europe, West Africa, Canary Islands, western Asia.
Height and spread: 30–90 x 45cm/12–36 x 18in.
Habit and form: Herbaceous perennial.
Leaf shape: Pinnatifid.
Pollinated: Insect.

Above: The blooms are a striking yellow.

Right: The long thin seed-heads are the so-called horns that give the plant its name.

Bleeding Heart
Lyre flower, *Dicentra spectabilis*

Distribution: China, north-eastern Asia.
Height and spread: 80 x 45cm/32 x 18in.
Habit and form: Herbaceous.
Leaf shape: Two-ternate, fern-like.
Pollinated: Insect.

Far right: The delicate, arching, stems are extremely striking.

The bleeding heart is named for its rosy heart-shaped flowers, with white inner petals, which dangle from arching stems. It grows in moist soils in light woodland cover, and is a particularly handsome plant, especially from mid-spring onwards, as the light green, deeply divided leaves emerge from the ground below the arching flower stems. It often dies down to ground level before the end of summer. All parts of the plant are mildly poisonous if ingested and can irritate the skin. An old English common name is "Lady in the Bath", referring to the appearance of the flower when turned upside down.

Identification: A clump-forming perennial with thick, fleshy roots and pale green, compound, almost fern-like leaves, 15–40cm/6–16in long, with oval, sometimes lobed leaflets. Arching, fleshy stems support arching racemes of pendent, heart-shaped flowers, 2–3cm/¾–1¼in long, with mid-pink outer petals and white inner ones, in late spring or early summer. The stems rarely persist for long past mid-summer and by late summer the entire plant dies down to ground level until the following spring.

PINKS AND GERANIUM FAMILIES

The Caryophyllaceae, or pinks, are herbs or rarely subshrubs. The flowers typically feature a corolla of five distinct, frequently clawed petals, and the common name "pink" is derived from a word meaning scalloped, characterizing the petal edges of many in this family. The Geraniaceae, or geraniums, are a varied family, featuring five-petalled flowers and a beaked fruit that often disperses the seed explosively.

Clove Pink

Carnation, *Dianthus caryophyllus*

This native of Eurasia has been cultivated since ancient times and there are classical Greek and Roman allusions to its use in garlands. The name *Dianthus* derives from the Greek *dios* (god) and *anthos* (flower), and literally means "flower of the gods". Despite its ancient history the wild form of this flower is rare and most wild populations are probably derived from cultivated stock.

Identification: Slightly woody perennial with glabrous and glaucous stems and leaves. The leaves are linear, flat and soft in texture and entire along the margins, with conspicuous sheaths around swollen nodes. The conspicuous, fragrant, mostly solitary flowers have five broad petals with toothed edges, mostly flesh-coloured or pink, and are produced in loose cymes on stiff, ascending stems during the summer months. A variable plant that is often the result of escape from cultivation from which many forms have been derived.

Left: The ragged petal edges appear zigzagged, hence the use of the word "clove" meaning divided in the common name.

Distribution: Eurasia: widely naturalized but rarely found wild except perhaps in some Mediterranean countries.
Height and spread: 30–60 x 25–30cm/12–24in x 10–12in.
Habit and form: Herbaceous perennial.
Leaf shape: Linear.
Pollinated: Moth and butterfly.

Meadow Cranesbill

Geranium pratense

This genus should not be confused with the showy geraniums grown in pots for greenhouse or home decoration, or for summer bedding, which are correctly known as pelargoniums. True geranium species, commonly known as cranesbills because of their beak-like seedpods, are a group of hardy perennials chiefly found in the temperate regions of Eurasia and North America. The meadow cranesbill is the most widespread and robust, with large, conspicuous blue flowers. The flowers are produced in abundance from early summer to mid-autumn.

Right: The large, blue flowers are followed by the long, pointed seedheads that give rise to the common name of cranesbill.

Identification: This hairy perennial, with a woody rootstock forming conspicuous clumps, has erect stems, which are sticky in the upper part, and long-stemmed, dark green leaves divided into seven to nine thin, toothed and divided segments. The 2.5–4cm/1–1½in saucer-shaped, pale violet-blue flowers are borne in clusters above the foliage. The flowers are followed by hairy, beak-like fruits, which curve down after flowering but become erect as they ripen. They have five segments that curl upwards explosively to disperse the seeds.

Right: The bright blue flowers are produced abundantly during the summer months.

Distribution: Europe.
Height and spread: 50cm/20n.
Habit and form: Herbaceous perennial.
Leaf shape: Palmate.
Pollinated: Bee or other insect.

Zonal Pelargonium

Pelargonium zonale

This plant, familiar in cultivation for growing in pots and bedding schemes, has its origins on the dry rocky hills, stony slopes and forest margins of South Africa, from the Southern Cape to Natal. The flowers of this strikingly beautiful species range from all shades of red to pink and pure white, and in its natural habitat it is an abundant and often conspicuous feature. *Pelargonium zonale* flowers throughout the year, with a peak in spring.

Left: The flowers are produced on conspicuous heads, ranging from red, through pink to pure white. The new growth of the characteristic "horseshoe-marked" leaves are the perfect foil for the flowers.

Far right: The flowerheads are produced so prolifically in spring.

Identification: This erect or scrambling, softly woody, evergreen shrub usually grows up to 90cm/3ft but can reach heights up to 3m/10ft. The young branches are almost succulent and usually covered with hairs, but harden with age. The large leaves are often smooth and a characteristic dark horseshoe-shaped mark is often present. The distinctly irregular flowers are borne in a typically umbel-like inflorescence.

Distribution: South Africa.
Height and spread: 90cm–3m/3–10ft.
Habit and form: Subshrub.
Leaf shape: Circular.
Pollinated: Insect.

OTHER PINKS AND GERANIUM SPECIES

Musk Storksbill *Erodium moschatum*
The purple flowers of this annual or biennial species from Europe are clustered in a flower-head at the top of the stems, from which develop long, pointed seedheads – hence the name. The somewhat fern-like leaves are hairy and slightly toothed.

Red Campion *Silene dioica*

A showy herbaceous perennial that is widespread and abundant, red campion is most often associated with woodland, shady places and hedgerows, although it can occur in open situations such as sea cliffs. It hybridizes quite freely with the related white campion, *S. latifolia*: the hybrids resemble red campion but are taller, with pale pink flowers.

Ragged Robin *Lychnis flos-cuculi*

With its apparently ragged, deeply lobed petals, ragged robin is one of the most attractive flowers of wet meadowland. Like other wetland plants, it has declined in recent years, as a result of habitat destruction by modern agricultural practices.

Corncockle

Agrostemma githago

This attractive and once common weed of cornfields has become rare in the wild due to modern agricultural practices. The flower is at first male, the anthers shedding their pollen before the stigmas are mature; these are arranged at the mouth of the tube so that the visiting butterflies push their faces among them and pick up pollen. A day or two later the flower "becomes" female and the stigmas occupy the mouth in the same way to receive pollen.

Identification: This annual herb has a tall, slender stem with a dense coat of white hairs. Narrow, lance-shaped leaves, 10–12.5cm/4–5in long, are produced in pairs and their stalkless bases meet around the stem. The large, solitary flowers, which appear from early to late summer, have very long stalks that issue from the leaf axils. The flowers are 4–5cm/1½–2in across, with purple, pale-streaked petals and a woolly calyx with five strong ridges and five long, green teeth that far exceed the length of the petals. The fruit is a sessile (stalkless) capsule, which opens with five teeth.

Distribution: Europe.
Height and spread: 60–150cm/2–5ft.
Habit and form: Annual.
Leaf shape: Lancoleate.
Pollinated: Insect.

Below: The long, green "teeth" of the woolly calyx exceed the length of the petals and give this flower a distinctive appearance.

PRIMULA AND DOGBANE FAMILIES

The Primulaceae, or primulas, occur mainly in temperate and mountainous regions of the Northern Hemisphere. Many species of Primula *are cultivated for their attractive flowers. The genera and species of the Apocynaceae (dogbane family) are distributed primarily in the tropics and subtropics and are poorly represented in temperate regions. Plants of the Apocynaceae are often poisonous.*

Primrose

Primula vulgaris

Without doubt this plant is one of the most attractive and best known of the primula family. It has long been cultivated and its name derives from the Latin *prima rosa* meaning "first rose". It frequently hybridizes with the related cowslip, *P. veris*, although the flowers remain pale yellow. Other colours arise through hybridization with cultivated stock.

Identification: The rootstock becomes knotty with the successive bases of fallen leaves and bears cylindrical, branched rootlets on all sides. The leaves are egg-shaped to oblong, about 12.5cm/5in long and 4cm/1½in across in the middle, smooth above with prominent, hairy veins and veinlets beneath, the margins irregularly toothed, tapering into a winged stalk. The fragrant flowers are pale yellow with a darker centre and sepals forming a bell-shaped, pleated tube. They appear from late winter to late spring, each borne on a separate stalk and followed by an egg-shaped capsule enclosed within a persistent calyx.

Above: The primrose is a woodland or hedgerow plant.

Left: The conspicuous flowers are held above a low rosette of shiny geen leaves.

Distribution: Europe.
Height and spread: 5–20cm/2–8in.
Habit and form: Herbaceous perennial.
Leaf shape: Obovate to oblong.
Pollinated: Insect.

Right: Pink flowers, growing wild are the result of crosses with cultivated plants.

Giant Cowslip

Primula florindae

The aptly named giant cowslip is native to south-east Xizang in Tibet, where it grows in marshes and along streams in the constantly waterlogged soils. The species was named by the renowned Himalayan plant explorer, Frank Kingdon-Ward, in honour of his wife Florinda. It was a true compliment as it is one of the most imposing wild primroses to be seen and is very fragrant. It requires a very moist, acidic soil and flowers mainly from early to late summer.

Above and left: The yellow or rarely red flowers have a sweet spicy scent.

Identification: Heart-shaped, toothed, shiny mid-green leaves with rounded tips, on stout winged stalks 4–20cm/ 1½–8in long and often tinged red, form large herbaceous rosettes below flowering stems that can reach 1m/3ft in height. Each inflorescence consists of up to 40 pendent, funnel-shaped, sulphur-yellow flowers, smelling strongly of nutmeg or cloves. Both the stems and flowers are farinose (dusted with a mealy coating) and the overall habit of the plant is quite robust.

Distribution: South-east Tibet.
Height and spread: Up to 90cm/3ft.
Habit and form: Herbaceous perennial.
Leaf shape: Ovate
Pollinated: Insect.

Left: The flowerheads are held high above a rosette of foliage.

Oleander

Rose bay, *Nerium oleander*

When oleander grows in the wild it occurs along watercourses, in gravel soils and damp ravines. It is widely cultivated, particularly in warm temperate and subtropical regions, where it grows in parks, gardens and along roadsides. It prefers dry, warm climates and may naturalize in such areas. The whole plant, including the sap, is toxic.

Distribution: North Africa, eastern Mediterranean and South-east Asia.
Height and spread: 4m/13ft.
Habit and form: Evergreen shrub.
Leaf shape: Lanceolate.
Pollinated: Insect.

Right: The individual flowers are five petalled and may be pink or white. They are highly fragrant.

Right: Oleander forms a loose, attractive, evergreen shrub that is widely cultivated for its appearance.

Identification: Oleander is a summer-flowering evergreen shrub with narrow, entire, short-stalked, leathery, dark or grey-green leaves, 10–23cm/4–9in long, with prominent midribs, usually arising from the stem in groups of three. The terminal flowerheads are usually pink or white; each five-petalled flower is about 5cm/2in in diameter and the throat is fringed with long, petal-like projections. The fruits are long, narrow capsules, 10–12.5cm/4–5in long and 6–8mm/¼–⅜in in diameter, which open to disperse fluffy seeds.

OTHER PRIMULA AND DOGBANE SPECIES

Cowslip *Primula veris*
This spring-flowering plant, appears at the same time as the primrose, but is not as widespread (or as conspicuous) as that plant. It has a tight rosette of small, deep green, crinkled leaves and drooping clusters of small delicately scented deep yellow flowers on tall 25cm/10in stems.

Madagascar Periwinkle *Catharanthus roseus*
An evergreen perennial 45–120cm/18–48in tall with flowers of white, pink and intermediate colours, above deep green, glossy, oval leaves. Originally a native of Madagascar, it is now widely naturalized in many tropical countries as a garden escapee.

Primula vialii
The pyramidal flowers of this highly unusual primula look like miniature red hot pokers. They are bicolored, with purple at the base and reddish fuchsia at the tip, borne on 40cm/16in stems during the summer months. It is originally native to China although it is now widely cultivated in gardens.

Yellow Loosestrife *Lysimachia punctata*
This erect-growing perennial from south-eastern and central Europe has lance- to elliptic-shaped, mid-green leaves that grow in whorls of three or four. The small, bright yellow flowers are borne in the leaf axils at the ends of the stems during the summer.

Ivy-leaved Cyclamen

Sowbread *Cyclamen hederifolium*

This pretty little cyclamen has a wide distribution stretching from south-eastern France, through central Europe, Greece (including Crete and many of the Aegean islands) and western Turkey. It inhabits woodland, scrub, and rocky hillsides from sea level to 1,300m/4,250ft, although its popularity in cultivation has led it to spread to other areas. The flowers are usually pink, but there is also a white-flowered form, though this is rare in the wild.

Identification: The pink flowers, with a purple-magenta, V-shaped blotch at the base of each petal, appear from mid- to late autumn. The leaves are very variable, and can be every shape from almost circular to lance-shaped. They vary from dull or bright plain green to plain silver with various forms of hastate (spear-shaped) pattern in between, with the pattern in silver, grey, cream or a different shade of green. The undersides can be green or purple-red.

Left: The flowers and foliage arise from a rounded tuber.

Distribution: Europe, chiefly the Mediterranean.
Height and spread: 15cm/6in.
Habit and form: Herbaceous perennial.
Leaf shape: Variable, chiefly ivy-shaped.
Pollinated: Insect.

Right: After flowering, the flower stalks coil down to the soil surface to deposit the seeds.

Below: The flowers mainly appear before the young leaves.

GENTIANS AND BELLFLOWERS

Worldwide, the Gentianaceae, or gentians, comprise mainly herbaceous perennials but also include a few shrubs or small trees, and are particularly well represented in mountain areas. The Campanulaceae, or bellflowers are herbs, shrubs, or rarely small trees, usually with milky sap, comprising about 70 genera and 2,000 species. Many of the species of both families are highly ornamental and familiar plants.

Stemless Gentian

Gentianella, *Gentiana acaulis*

In the wild this gentian grows in the Alps and Carpathian Mountains in dry acid grasslands, bogs, on rubble and scree slopes and occasionally in alpine woods, at elevations of 1,400–3,000m/4,600–9,850ft. Although it usually grows in acid soils it can sometimes also be found on chalky limestone or sandstone. Its intense blue, funnel-shaped flowers, which almost obscure the foliage, make it one of the showiest alpine plants that can be seen in Europe, when it appears in early summer.

Right: The low mat of foliage can be inconspicuous until the flowers appear in early summer.

Identification: The leaves in the basal rosette are 2.5–4cm/1–1½in long, lance- to egg-shaped and glossy dark green. On the short flower stems the leaves are smaller and broader. The solitary 5cm/2in trumpet-shaped, lobed flowers are vivid dark blue, spotted green within. They are produced terminally on short stalks in spring and early summer and are followed by stalked, ellipsoid seed capsules.

Distribution: Europe, Spain to the Balkans.
Height and spread: 10 x 100cm/4 x 39in.
Habit and form: Slow-growing perennial.
Leaf shape: Lanceolate.
Pollinated: Bee and butterfly.

Autumn-flowering Gentian

Gentiana sino-ornata

This plant, discovered by the Scots plant hunter George Forrest in 1904 in south-west China, yields the richest tones of blue trumpets among the fallen leaves of late autumn. It is a native of north-west Yunnan and adjacent Tibet, and grows in wet ground. It prefers a rich acid soil, which drains well but will hold moisture, and is often found growing in well-oxygenated, moving water. The flowers exhibit a range of colour from royal blue to purple-blue, interspersed with greenish-yellow bands.

Identification: The stems of this prostrate perennial, 15–20cm/6–8in long, ascend at the tips and root at nodes. The basal leaves form loose rosettes; on the stems the dark green leaves are paired, narrowly lance-shaped, about 4cm/1½in long. The deep blue, tubular flowers, up to 5cm/2in across, are borne singly on the ends of the stems, with lobes twice the length of the tube. They have five bands of deep purple-blue, panelled green-white, on the outside and are paler within, sometimes with a streaked throat.

Right: The bright blue flowers appear at the end of the stems in damp acidic soils and give a stunning autumnal display.

Distribution: South-west China and Tibet.
Height and spread: 15–20cm/6–8in.
Habit and form: Prostrate herbaceous perennial.
Leaf shape: Lanceolate.
Pollinated: Insect.

Yellow Wort

Blackstonia perfoliata

Distribution: Europe.
Height and spread:
45cm/18in.
Habit and form: Herbaceous
perennial.
Leaf shape: Ovate, appearing
perfoliate on flower stems.
Pollinated: Insect.

Yellow wort is an almost unmistakable plant that is able to grow in very alkaline soil. It is most commonly found growing on dry grassland over shallow chalk, limestone soils and occasionally on dunes. The eight-petalled, yellow flowers close in the afternoon and the waxy blue-green leaves are highly distinctive. The plant was given its botanical name in honour of an 18th-century London apothecary and botanist, John Blackstone.

Left: The basal rosette is inconspicuous when growing in grassland but the distinctive, blue-green, tall, upright stems with their encircling, slightly cup-shaped leaves are unmistakable.

Identification: The oval leaves, which are bluish-green and hairless, are stalkless and form a loose rosette at the base of the stem. The leaves on the stem are in pairs with their bases fused together, making it appear as if the stem passes through the middle of a single leaf. Between early summer and mid-autumn the yellow flowers appear on 45cm/18in stems. They have eight petals, joined at the base to form a short tube.

Below: The tight, green buds give rise to showy, yellow blooms.

OTHER GENTIANS AND BELLFLOWERS

Sea Rose *Orphium frutescens*
The glossy pink stars of this bushy, evergreen perennial always attract attention, especially when the surrounding vegetation goes brown and dormant. The sea rose is found in South Africa, along the south-west coast of the Cape, growing in clumps on sandy flats and marshes.

Feverwort *Centaurium erythraea*
The feverwort is a small, erect annual or biennial herb that is indigenous to Europe, western Asia and North Africa, and has become naturalized in North America. The stem grows up to 30cm/12in high and is topped with numerous pink or red flowers. It favours dry, shady banks, waysides and pastures.

Bonnet Bellflower *Codonopsis ovata*
This plant from the western Himalayas has small, oval, greyish and somewhat downy leaves, and two or more flowers on a stem. The drooping, bell-shaped flowers appear from early summer; they are pale greyish-blue with purple reticulations and an orange-and-white base inside.

Harebell *Campanula rotundifolia*
This little wildflower is found beside streams, on heaths and moors, and in grassy places. It has a basal rosette of rounded or kidney-shaped leaves, with smaller thin, pointed leaves up the stem, and large, pale blue bellflowers.

Peach-leaved Bellflower

Campanula persicifolia

The peach-leaved bellflower is an extremely pretty wildflower noted for its tall, thin stems with a few scattered leaves, and large, open bellflowers, which are borne freely during the summer months. It was at one time grown as a culinary vegetable, but is now more commonly grown as an ornamental plant, this having led to its occurrence as a garden escapee in many areas. The plant prefers well-drained, alkaline soils and can grow in light woodland or open situations such as grassland.

Identification: The plant is a rosette-forming perennial with slender, white rhizomes and evergreen, narrow basal leaves, which are lance-shaped to oblong or oval, toothed, bright green and 10–15cm/4–6in long. Short terminal racemes of two or three, occasionally solitary, slightly pendent, cup-shaped flowers up to 5cm/2in across, varying from white to lilac-blue, are produced on slender stems or from the leaf axils, in early or midsummer. The seeds ripen from late summer to mid-autumn.

Distribution: Europe to western and northern Asia.
Height and spread: 100 x 45cm/39 x 18in.
Habit and form: Herbaceous perennial.
Leaf shape: Lanceolate.
Pollinated: Bee, fly, beetle, moth and butterfly.

Below: The tall, thin, showy flower stems support numerous open, slightly pendent, blue bellflowers.

EUPHORBIA AND ASPHODEL FAMILIES

The Euphorbiaceae, or euphorbias, are one of the largest families of herbs, shrubs, and trees, generally characterized by the occurrence of milky, often toxic sap. They are mostly monoecious (bearing flowers of both sexes on one plant) and sometimes succulent and cactus-like. The Asphodelaceae, or asphodels, range in size from minute succulents to large trees, and the family is generally quite diverse in form.

Wood Spurge

Robb's euphorbia, *Euphorbia amygdaloides* var. *robbiae*

The wood spurge is an attractive perennial plant of broadleaved woodland and shady banks. It spreads by underground runners until eventually the evergreen leaves form a low carpet over the ground, smothering smaller plants. Upright spikes of lime-green flowers emerge in spring and persist through early summer. The species is widespread across Europe, with this subspecies being restricted to north-west Turkey. The species has become popular in cultivation and can often be found outside its natural geographical range.

Identification: This bushy, softly hairy, evergreen perennial has reddish-green, biennial stems and spoon- to egg-shaped, leathery leaves, 2.5–7.5cm/1–3in long. The leaves are shiny dark green, becoming much darker in winter, and are closely set on the stems. From mid-spring to early summer it bears terminal flattened flower clusters, 18cm/7in tall, of greenish-yellow cyathia (groups of male and female flowers lacking petals and sepals) surrounded by cup-shaped bracts.

Distribution: North-west Turkey.
Height and spread: 60 x 30cm/24 x 12in.
Habit and form: Evergreen perennial.
Leaf shape: Obovate.
Pollinated: Insect.

Above left: The greenish-yellow cup-shaped flowers.

Left: The flowers are held in spikes.

Castor Oil Plant

Ricinus communis

This fast-growing species, originally a native of north-eastern Africa to western Asia, has long been cultivated both for its ornamental value and also for the castor oil yielded by the seeds, which are highly toxic. As a result, the plant's range has been greatly extended and it is now a common wayside species in many tropical and subtropical locations worldwide.

Identification: The succulent stem is 7.5–15cm/3–6in in diameter, and very variable in all aspects. The smooth leaves are alternately arranged, circular, palmately compound. The flowers are numerous in long inflorescences, with male flowers at the base and red female flowers at the tips; there are no petals in either sex, but three to five greenish sepals. The flower is followed by a round fruit capsule, 2.5cm/1in in diameter, on an elongated stalk that is usually spiny. The fruit is green at first, ripening to brown, and usually contains three attractively mottled seeds.

Right: The flowerheads have male flowers at the base, and female flowers at the top.

Below: The leaves are 15–45cm/6–18in long, with 6–11 toothed lobes.

Distribution: Probably native to Africa, but widely cultivated.
Height and spread: Up to 10–13m/33–42ft.
Habit and form: Shrubby perennial.
Leaf shape: Palmate.
Pollinated: Insect.

Krantz Aloe

Aloe arborescens

Distribution: Southern Africa.
Height and spread: 2–3m/6½–10ft.
Habit and form: Shrubby succulent.
Leaf shape: Sickle-shaped and rounded.
Pollinated: Bird (particularly sunbird), bee.

The krantz aloe is a distinctive species that develops into a multi-headed shrub with striking grey-green leaves, armed with conspicuous pale teeth, arranged in attractive rosettes. It is most closely related to the smaller, but somewhat similar, *Aloe mutabilis*, which can generally be distinguished by its red-and-yellow flowers and broader leaves.

Identification: The succulent, greyish-green to bright green, sickle-shaped leaves, borne in rosettes, vary considerably in length but average 50–60cm/20–24in. The leaf margins are commonly armed with firm teeth, which are white or the same colour as the leaves. There is also a form with smooth margins. Two or more flower spikes up to 90cm/3ft long arise from each rosette in late winter and spring, usually simple but occasionally with up to two side branches. The scarlet, orange, pink or yellow flowers are borne in conical racemes and are rich in nectar.

Below: The rosettes of bluish-green, spine-edged leaves can form dense thickets in time, topped with attractive heads of tubular, pink or orange flower-heads, made up of single spikes.

OTHER EUPHORBIAS AND ASPHODELS

Basketball Euphorbia *Euphorbia obesa*

This slow-growing, ball-shaped plant is a native of South Africa's Great Karoo. It consists of a single, smooth-bodied, spineless, olive-green, swollen stem, covered in mauve to pale green striped markings. As it matures it becomes slightly columnar rather than globular. Flowers are produced in summer near the growing tip.

Indian Acalypha *Acalypha indica*

Also known as the Indian copperleaf, this erect annual herb grows up to 75cm/30in. It has numerous long, angular branches covered with soft hair and thin, smooth, egg-shaped leaves. The flowers are borne in long, erect spikes, and are followed by small, hairy fruits and minute, pale brown seeds.

Aloe vera

This succulent aloe is almost stalkless. Its pea-green leaves, spotted with white when young,  are 30–50cm/12–20in long and 10cm/4in broad at the base. Bright yellow, tubular flowers,25–35cm/ 10–14in long, are arranged in a slender, loose spike. This plant has long been cultivated for medicinal use and its exact origin is a mystery.

Red Hot Poker

Kniphofia caulescens

Red hot pokers are more often orange than red but resemble the colour of glowing embers nonetheless. They are a distinctive group of plants, with their strong outlines making them instantly recognizable. They are frequented by nectar-feeding birds, such as sunbirds and sugarbirds, as well as certain insects. The genus *Kniphofia* is very closely related to the genus *Aloe*. As a result, the first *Kniphofia* to be described, *K. uvaria*, was initially named *Aloe uvaria*. *K. caulescens* is notable for its stems, which become woody, giving it the appearance of a small shrub. It is a widely cultivated plant that may occur as a garden escapee far outside its natural range.

Below: Red hot pokers are clump-forming.

Distribution: Eastern South Africa.
Height and spread: 90cm/3ft or more.
Habit and form: Slightly woody herbaceous perennial.
Leaf shape: Linear.
Pollinated: Bird, sometimes insect.

Identification: The plant is an evergreen perennial with short, thick, woody-based stems and arching, linear, keeled, finely toothed, glaucous leaves, purple at the base. Coral-red flowers fading to pale yellow, 2.5cm/1in long with protruding stamens, are borne in short, cylindrical racemes on 1.2m/4ft stems from summer to autumn.

STONE PLANTS AND CRASSULAS

The Aizoaceae, or stone family, is particularly strongly represented in southern Africa. Many of its species are decorative, so are widely cultivated and some have become naturalized outside their normal range. The Crassulaceae, or crassulas, are mostly succulents, with flowers that are very similar to those of members of the rose and saxifrage families.

Houseleek

Hens and chicks, *Sempervivum tectorum*

This commonly cultivated perennial succulent plant is very occasionally found as a persistent colonist of old walls. It was formerly also frequent on thatched roofs of houses, but is now rarely found in this habitat. The genus *Sempervivum* comprises a range of succulent, rosette-forming, evergreen perennials that originate in the mountainous areas of Europe, central Asia and North Africa, often growing in crevices in the rocks. The plant requires well-drained soil and can tolerate drought. Each rosette is monocarpic (it blooms once and then dies).

Identification: An evergreen, mat-forming, succulent perennial, it has open rosettes up to 10cm/4in across of thick, oval to narrowly oblong, bristle-tipped leaves, to 4cm/1½in long, blue-green often suffused red-purple. Leaves often show seasonal variations in colour. In early to midsummer, it bears cymes, 5–10cm/2–4in across, of red-purple flowers on upright, hairy stems growing to 15cm/6in tall. The seeds ripen from mid- to late summer.

Left: The fleshy rosettes form are tightly packed.

Left: Each red-purple flower has numerous petals.

Right: One flowerhead arises from the centre of the rosette.

Distribution: French and Italian Alps.
Height and spread: 10–30cm/4–12in.
Habit and form: Succulent, evergreen, rosette-forming perennial.
Leaf shape: Obovate to narrowly oblong.
Pollinated: Insect.

Silver Jade Tree

Crassula arborescens

Found on granite or in quartzite areas, this distinctive, large, shrubby succulent is perfectly at home growing between boulders or in crevices. The plants are mainly found in areas of winter rainfall and are very tolerant of drought. The species has a scattered distribution in South Africa, from the Little Karoo to the Hex River Valley.

Right: The flowers appear in autumn to winter.

Below: Though tree-like it is actually a shrub.

Identification: Cylindrical branches bear grey-green leaves, tinged purple, to 7.5cm/3in long, with red margins that continue down both sides of the leaf. The leaves are oval, with rounded tips, tapering below, with entire margins; leaf stalks are absent or very short. The old leaves gradually become deciduous. The succulent stems are up 12.5cm/5in in diameter, frequently branched, and older specimens have peeling bark. The grey flowers are tinged pink at the tips, with five to seven petals, which are borne on long flower stalks.

Right: The pale grey-blue colour is in part due to the grey bloom that is naturally present.

Distribution: South Africa.
Height and spread: 4m/13ft.
Habit and form: Shrubby succulent.
Leaf shape: Ovate.
Pollinated: Insect.

OTHER STONE PLANTS AND CRASSULAS

Lithops terricolor
These so-called "living stones" have evolved to survive dry conditions while also evading detection by browsing animal species. They are masters of deception, producing pairs of stone-shaped succulent leaves that resemble the pieces of quartz among which they grow.

Conophytum minutum
A species of succulent plants native to the winter-rainfall deserts of South Africa and Namibia. They are commonly known as stone plants because of their cryptically mineralesque appearance until the autumn, when the first rains stimulate the appearance of pink-lavender or white flowers.

Rosea Ice Plant *Drosanthemum floribundum*
This ground-hugging perennial, with small, stubby, light green, succulent leaves, produces dazzling metallic-purple flowers each spring. It is known to survive in very hot, dry conditions and easily colonizes large, flat, open spaces in South Africa's Little Karoo, with one plant covering an area as large as 2sq m/22sq ft.

Stonecrop *Sedum acre*
A loosely tufted, mat-forming, evergreen perennial, widespread through much of Europe, the Mediterranean region and Turkey and naturalized in the eastern USA. Its bright yellow flowers appear in small cymes from early to mid-summer. It thrives in dry gravel soils and is drought tolerant.

Hottentot Fig

Ice plant, pigface, *Carpobrotus edulis*

A vigorous, prostrate plant, rooting as it spreads, with flowers that open only in the afternoon, the so-called hottentot fig is an immensely showy plant when encountered *en masse* and is extremely tolerant of maritime exposure. Although it was originally restricted to coastal and exposed areas around the South African coast, human activities have resulted in it spreading over large parts of Australia, southern Europe and California, where conditions are similar to those in its original home.

Identification: The stems are spreading or prostrate, up to 2m/6½ft long, 8–12mm/⅜–½in thick, with two cleft angles; flowering shoots have two fleshy internodes. The three-sided leaves are 4–7.5cm/1½–3in long, 8–15mm/⅜–⅝in wide, bright green, often tinged red along the edges; the upper surfaces are distinctly concave, causing them to curl slightly inwards; the keel is minutely toothed. Daisy-like flowers, 7–9cm/2¾–3½in across, open after noon in sun in spring and summer; they are yellow at first, becoming flesh coloured to pink, usually densely streaked when dry. Fig-like, edible fruits follow the flowers.

Distribution: Cape Province, South Africa.
Height and spread: 10 x 90cm/4 x 36in.
Habit and form: Mat-forming succulent perennial.
Leaf shape: Triangular.
Pollinated: Insect.

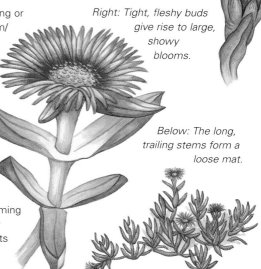

Right: Tight, fleshy buds give rise to large, showy blooms.

Below: The long, trailing stems form a loose mat.

Tiger's Jaws

Faucaria tigrina

This interesting little succulent, commonly known as tiger's jaws (the genus name *Faucaria* is derived from the Latin for "jaws") due to the teeth-like structures on the leaves, is a native of South Africa. The triangular leaves with pointed fleshy parts, are concave on the upper part, making them look like open jaws.

Identification: The plant forms succulent rosettes of triangular to diamond-shaped or oval leaves, tapered on the upper surface with very rounded lower surfaces, with the tips pulled forward and chin-like. The leaves are grey-green with numerous white dots arranged in rows and nine to ten stout, recurved, hair-tipped teeth along each margin.

Distribution: Eastern Cape Province, South Africa.
Height and spread: 10 x 50cm/4 x 20in.
Habit and form: Low shrubby succulent.
Leaf shape: Triangular to rhombic.
Pollinated: Insect.

Above: The plant builds woody stems with age and tolerates very droughty conditions.

Far left and left: Large, stalkless, daisy-like, yellow flowers, 5cm/2in across, are produced in late summer and early autumn.

SAXIFRAGE AND VIOLET FAMILIES

The Saxifragaceae, or saxifrage family, include herbaceous perennials and deciduous shrubs. In cultivation the family includes food and ornamental plants, although in the wild they are typical of arctic and boreal regions. The violet family is widely distributed in temperate and tropical regions of the world: the northern species are herbaceous, while others, abundant natives of tropical areas, are trees and shrubs.

Purple Mountain Saxifrage

Saxifraga oppositifolia

The purple saxifrage is frequently found on damp mountain rocks. It also sometimes grows at the foot of a mountain, from seeds washed down by fast-flowing streams, but rarely persists here as it is easily out-competed by other vegetation. It is an extremely widespread species, stretching from the Arctic down into the mountains of Europe, western Asia and North America. It tends to be variable due to the environmental variance across its large range. The plant is well known for its ability to flower very early in the year, but may produce a few additional flowers later in the summer. The flower colour is unusual among wild saxifrages.

Identification: A flat, mat-forming, opposite-leaved saxifrage, it has rosettes of stiff, oblong or elliptic, dark green leaves, to 5mm/⅕in long, on branching stems. The leaves are very densely packed and often secrete lime at the tips, giving the appearance of white flecks. In early summer, the plant bears solitary, almost stemless, cup-shaped, deep red-purple to pale pink or rarely white flowers, to 2cm/¾in across.

Below right: This tiny plant flowers profilically in spring and early summer.

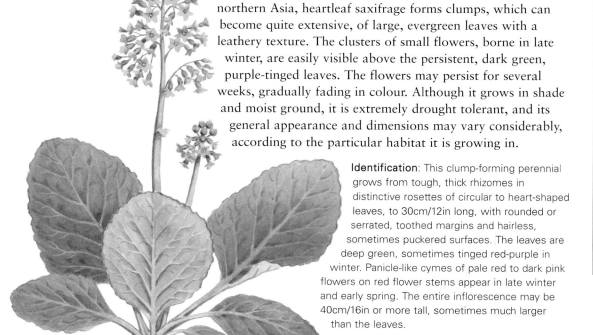

Distribution: Arctic, Eurasia and North America.
Height and spread: 2.5 x 20cm/1 x 8in or more.
Habit and form: Mat-forming, evergreen perennial.
Leaf shape: Oblong to elliptic.
Pollinated: Insect.

Heartleaf Saxifrage

Elephant's ears, *Bergenia cordifolia*

Found chiefly in damp, rocky woodland and meadows in northern Asia, heartleaf saxifrage forms clumps, which can become quite extensive, of large, evergreen leaves with a leathery texture. The clusters of small flowers, borne in late winter, are easily visible above the persistent, dark green, purple-tinged leaves. The flowers may persist for several weeks, gradually fading in colour. Although it grows in shade and moist ground, it is extremely drought tolerant, and its general appearance and dimensions may vary considerably, according to the particular habitat it is growing in.

Identification: This clump-forming perennial grows from tough, thick rhizomes in distinctive rosettes of circular to heart-shaped leaves, to 30cm/12in long, with rounded or serrated, toothed margins and hairless, sometimes puckered surfaces. The leaves are deep green, sometimes tinged red-purple in winter. Panicle-like cymes of pale red to dark pink flowers on red flower stems appear in late winter and early spring. The entire inflorescence may be 40cm/16in or more tall, sometimes much larger than the leaves.

Distribution: Siberia and Mongolia.
Height and spread: 40cm/16in or more.
Habit and form: Evergreen perennial.
Leaf shape: Rounded to heart-shaped.
Pollinated: Insect.

Heartsease

Wild pansy, *Viola tricolor*

Distribution: Eurasia from the Arctic to the southern Mediterranean.
Height and spread: 5–15 x 30cm/2–6 x 12in or more.
Habit and form: Annual or short-lived herbaceous perennial.
Leaf shape: Lanceolate to ovate.
Pollinated: Insect, especially bumblebee.

The heartsease is a variable species but it may always be readily distinguished from the other violets by the general form of its foliage, which is very deeply cut. The species is an annual or short-lived perennial, but crosses from it and other species have given rise to garden pansies. It is very widely distributed, and is found from the Arctic to North Africa and north-west India. Several varieties have been distinguished as subspecies.

Identification: The stems are generally very angular, erect to ascending and free branching. The leaves are deeply cut into rounded lobes, the terminal one being largest, with blunt tips and round-toothed margins; the upper leaves are lance-shaped to oval. The flat-faced flowers, 6mm–3cm/¼–1¼in across, vary a great deal in size and colour: they are purple, yellow or white, and most commonly a combination of all three. The upper petals are generally the most showy and purple, with the lowest and broadest petal usually yellow. The base of the lowest petal is elongated into a spur, as in the violet.

Below: The small, usually tricoloured flowers vary in colour.

OTHER SAXIFRAGE AND VIOLETS

Saxifraga fortunei
A deciduous perennial herb from Japan, with large panicles of white blossoms that rise in profusion on 50cm/20in red stems from rosettes of handsome, large, dark green, glossy, rounded leaves during the autumn.

Astilbe chinensis
This herbaceous perennial from China and Korea reaches 70cm/28in and is at its most handsome when the short, white, flushed pink or magenta flower panicles arise above the coarse mid- to light green foliage during the summer months.

Viola cornuta
The strong purple flowers of this plant emerge from early to late summer. It originated in the Pyrenees, and is found in pastures and rocky grassland on calcareous soils at 700–2,300m/2,300–7,500ft. It was once used extensively in crosses with Victorian pansy stock to introduce its vigorous tufted growth and perennial habit to cultivars.

Golden Saxifrage *Chrysosplenium oppositifolium*
From mid-spring until midsummer the tiny flowers of this low, slightly hairy, creeping perennial deck roadside ditches and other damp places. The flower petals are golden green and the young, stalked, wavy-edged, evergreen, opposite leaves are similar, so may not easily be seen.

Sweet Violet

Viola odorata

The classic florist's violet, the sweet violet was exported widely from Europe in colonial times as it was a popular cut flower in the late 19th and early 20th centuries. It is highly fragrant, and on a still day its scent can be detected before the flower is seen. It is the parent of many violet cultivars, and is still grown commercially.

Identification: Robust, prostrate stolons creep and spread this stemless, perennial plant. The leaves are heart-shaped, with scalloped or slightly serrated edges, dark green, smooth, sometimes downy underneath; they arise alternately from stolons, forming a basal rosette. Flower stalks arise from the leaf axils from early spring to early summer, each bearing a single deep purple, blue to pinkish or even yellow-white bloom. The flower is five-petalled, the lower petal lengthened into a hollow spur beneath and the lateral petals with a hairy centre line, with a pair of scaly bracts placed a little above the middle of the stalk. In autumn, small, insignificant flowers, without petals and scent, produce abundant seed.

Distribution: Europe.
Height and spread: 15cm/6in.
Habit and form: Herbaceous perennial.
Leaf shape: Heart-shaped.
Pollinated: Insect, especially bee.

Right: The seed capsule splits into three when ripe.

Below: The showy, fragrant, mostly blue flowers give this plant its name.

CARROT FAMILY

The Apiaceae, or carrot family, are mostly temperate herbs, with the highest diversity in the northern, world and tropical uplands. They are characterized by flowers in umbels, hollow stems and sheathing flower stalks. Many species are important as food crops, and for aromatic compounds that are used as spices, although this usage masks the fact that the majority of species in this family are highly toxic.

Sea holly

Eryngium alpinum

There are more than 200 species of *Eryngium* or sea holly as it is more commonly known, and while they do not all come from maritime locations, they do all share a tendency to grow on very well drained sites. This particular species looks rather like a teasel (*Dipsacus* spp.), although it is not related at all. Its tough, bright green, veined basal leaves become more and more pointed and divided as they go up the stem, and end in a ruff of spiky bracts that look like steely blue feathers, inside which is the matching domed flowerhead.

Identification: A perennial with basal rosette of leaves, 7.5–15cm/3–6in long, that are persistent and ovate to triangular-cordate, spiny toothed and soft. The upper leaves are more rounded, palmately lobed and blue tinged. The cylindrical-ovoid disc of sessile flowers comprises 25 or more small steel-blue or white flowers held among spiny bracts. These are followed by small, scaly fruits.

Distribution: West and central Balkans.
Height and spread: 45cm/18in.
Habit and form: Herbaceous perennial.
Leaf shape: Rounded.
Pollinated: Bees.

Left and far left: The "teasel-like" flowers are held high above the basal rosette of leaves.

Fennel

Foeniculum vulgare

Fennel is a well known culinary herb, often grown in gardens and as a consequence it has been spread far beyond its original range. It is found naturally in the Mediterranean areas of Europe where it grows in dry, stony calcareous soils near the sea, and while it is in leaf all year, it is chiefly noticed when the scented flowers appear from August to October. It often has a coastal distribution, though it cannot stand high wind so is usually found a little way inland.

Identification: A slender, glaucescent, aromatic perennial or biennial growing to 2m/6½ft with soft, hollow stems that are finely striate, ascending and branching alternately at flowering. The leaves, to 30cm/12in, have sheathing bases and are triangular in outline, 3–4 pinnate and extremely finely cut with segments. The flowers appear in the summer and are in compound umbels, 10–40 rayed, bisexual and yellow; followed by ovoid-oblong, ridged fruits.

Below: The seedheads.

Left: The flat, greenish-yellow flower umbels (right) are followed by rounded, flattened seeds (far left).

Distribution: Europe.
Height and spread: 2m/6½ft.
Habit and form: Herbaceous perennial.
Leaf shape: Pinnate (filiform).
Pollinated: Insect, especially bees and flies.

Left: The tall flowering stems are very striking although the plant often goes unnoticed when not in flower.

Ground elder

Aegopodium podagraria, Goutweed, Bishop's weed

This small herbaceous plant is common in hedgerows and cultivated land and a common garden weed. Ground elder was once greatly valued as a pot herb, and for its medicinal qualities, leading to its being transported well outside its natural range, where it has since become a problem plant. The large, pretty, white flowers appear in early to midsummer and in warmer regions are followed by flattened seed vessels, which when ripe are detached and blown about by the wind.

Distribution: Europe, often spread further by cultivation.
Height and spread: 70cm/28in.
Habit and form: Herbaceous perennial.
Leaf shape: Bipinnate.
Pollinated: Insects, especially bees.

Right: The pretty white umbels of this flower are very noticeable and appear around midsummer.

Identification: A herbaceous plant with stems arising from elongated rhizomes and fibrous roots, multiple from the base, with a strong scent, glabrous, to 70cm/28in tall. Basal leaves are long petiolate, bipinnately divided with long petiole, leaflets mostly glabrous or with a few short stiff hairs on the main veins below, ovate to oblong, serrate to doubly serrate. Small, five-petalled, white flowers appear in terminal pedunculate compound umbels. Fruits are slightly compressed, ellipsoid, glabrous, with a conspicuous groove although they are only viable in warmer regions.

Great masterwort
Astrantia major

This clump-forming perennial has rounded flowerheads, surrounded by papery, whitish, faintly pink bracts. It is found in moist woodlands and on the banks of streams in sub-alpine regions across central and eastern Europe.

Cow parsley *Anthriscus sylvestris*
This familiar plant of European temperate woodland edge, wayside and pasture looks very similar to some poisonous species so care must be taken when identifying it. Its large white umbels are extremely showy and often form a major constituent of unimproved grassland.

Carom *Trachyspermum ammi*
An important source of an aromatic spice, carom is very common to Indian and African cuisine. It closely resembles thyme in flavour. India is one of the most important sources of the plant, although it is probably of eastern Mediterranean origin, perhaps from Egypt.

Wild carrot *Daucus carota*
This flower occurs naturally on cultivated and wasteland, among grass, especially by the sea and on chalk, throughout Europe, parts of Asia and North Africa. It has long been domesticated for human use.

Parsley

Petroselinum crispum

Parsley was native to central and southern Europe although cultivation of the plant for use as a herb has led to its becoming widely naturalized elsewhere, especially within the temperate regions fo the Northern Hemisphere. The plant naturally inhabits grassy places, walls, rocky outcrops and dry hedgerow banks. It is a biennial herb that is in flower from June to August, displaying tiny, star-shaped, green-yellow flowers in flat-topped umbels.

Identification: A stout, erect glabrous biennial, with a clean, pungent smell when crushed. Stems are solid and striate, with branches ascending. The three-pinnate leaves are bright green, with 4–12 pairs that are ovate in outline, cuneate at the base and toothed, with a long petiole. The upper cauline leaves are small. Yellowish flowers appear in flat-topped, compound umbels, to 5cm/2in across in summer, followed by small, rounded flattened seeds. Oblong, greyish-brown fruits 3mm/⅛in long, with spines on the curved surface, ripen from late summer to early autumn.

Distribution: Southeast Europe, Sardinia.
Height and spread: 30–75cm/12–30in.
Habit and form: Biennial.
Leaf shape: Pinnate.
Pollinated: Insect, especially flies.

Above right and right: The small, greenish-yellow flowerheads can easily be overlooked in the wild when plants grow among other vegetation.

BORAGE AND LOBELIA FAMILIES

The Boraginaceae are herbs, shrubs or trees that are found worldwide in tropical, subtropical and temperate areas but are most concentrated in the Mediterranean region. The Lobeliaceae family contains flowering plants native to both hemispheres, including annual and perennial herbs, shrubs and trees. The family is included by some authorities in the bellflower family, Campanulaceae.

Green Alkanet

Evergreen bugloss, *Pentaglottis sempervirens*

Green alkanet is a member of the forget-me-not family, but it is unusual in that the flowers do not grow in a curved spike as in most members of the family. The plant is native to south-west Europe, but is now naturalized in hedge banks and woodland edges in many areas outside this range. It is especially common close to towns and villages, probably due to its having been used at one time as the source of a red dye that was extracted from the roots. It can grow in deep woodland shade or open positions, although it usually requires moist soil and is common in damp, shady places, or by roads and in hedges, near the sea.

Identification: A coarsely hairy, taprooted perennial, with strong, erect to ascending, fairly leafy stems, arises from a basal rosette of pointed, oval to oblong, rough-hairy, mid-green leaves, 10–40cm/4–16in long; the stem leaves are rather smaller. From spring to early summer, it bears small leafy clusters of bright blue flowers, to 12mm/½in across, with stamens hidden inside the short, narrow flower-tube, five spreading lobes and a white eye.

Right: The small seedhead contains numerous seeds.

Left: Tall flower stems arise from the spreading leafy base.

Right: The flowers are eyecatching.

Distribution: Western Europe.
Height and spread: 30cm–1m/12–39in.
Habit and form: Herbaceous perennial.
Leaf shape: Ovate.
Pollinated: Insect.

Common Borage

Borago officinalis

Borage is a hardy annual with obscure origins. It grows wild from central Europe to the western Mediterranean but has been used by people for so long that it is now naturalized in most parts of Europe; mostly near dwellings. It has been grown as a herb – the leaves taste like cucumber, despite their texture – and for its flowers, which yield excellent honey. The numerous bright blue flowers, held in loose, branching heads appear from late spring onward.

Below: Borage has a messy straggly habit.

Above and far right: The showy, star-shaped flowerheads sport numerous blue flowers, and are favoured by bees.

Identification: Borage is a robust, freely branching annual, with lance-shaped to oval, dull green leaves up to 15cm/6in long, covered with white, stiff, prickly hairs. The leaf margins are entire, but wavy. The round stems, 60cm/2ft high, are branched, hollow and succulent, with alternate, stalkless, lance-shaped leaves, supporting branched clusters of five-petalled, star-shaped, bright blue flowers up to 2.5cm/1in across, over a long period in summer. The flowers are easily distinguished from those of every other plant in this order by their prominent black anthers, which form a cone in the centre. The fruit consists of four brownish-black nutlets.

Distribution: Central Europe, though widely naturalized elsewhere.
Height and spread: 60cm/2ft.
Habit and form: Annual.
Leaf shape: Ovate to lanceolate.
Pollinated: Bee.

Giant Lobelia

Lobelia deckenii

The giant lobelia grows on Kilimanjaro in Kenya, between 3,700–4,300m/12,000–14,000ft, in an alpine region dominated by small shrubs. The plant is endemic to the area and exceptionally striking. In order to protect the sensitive leaf buds from the sub-zero night-time temperatures, it closes its leaves around the central core while the covered rosettes secrete a slimy solution that helps to insulate and preserve them. It is pollinated by birds, especially the brightly coloured sunbirds that inhabit the area. Several related subspecies exist on the mountains of East Africa, including *L. deckenii* ssp. *keniensis* on Mount Kenya. The plants are monocarpic – each rosette dying after flowering – but are characterized by extremely long lifespans.

Distribution: Restricted to a few east African mountains.
Height and spread: Up to 3m/10ft or more.
Habit and form: Rosette-forming evergreen perennial.
Leaf shape: Ovate to oblong.
Pollinated: Bird.

Right: Each flower is shaped for the bills of visiting sunbirds that feed on the rich nectar.

Identification: The thick, hollow flower stem, growing up to 3m/10ft, arises out of the centre of a tight rosette of leaves that are broadly oval to oblong, glaucous to shiny, strongly ridged down the midrib on the lower side, with clearly defined veination at almost right angles to the midrib. In immature specimens, the rosette of leaves is arranged in a tight spiral, with a cabbage-like central bud. The flower spike is covered with spiralling, triangular bracts that conceal blue flowers.

OTHER BORAGE AND LOBELIA SPECIES

Viper's Bugloss
Echium vulgare
A European native, viper's bugloss is a bushy, upright biennial with narrowly lance-shaped to linear,

toothed, white, bristly-hairy leaves. In early summer it produces short, dense spikes of bell-shaped flowers, blue in bud but ranging from purple or vibrant blue to pink or white.

Siberian Bugloss *Brunnera macrophylla*
A native of woodlands in the Caucasus. Its leaves, up to 15cm/6in across, are roughly kidney shaped and provide an attractive foil for the sprays of starry, pale blue, forget-me-not-like flowers that appear shortly after the leaves.

Scrambling Gromwell *Lithodora diffusa*
Native to France, Spain and Portugal, this plant is recognized by its sprawling habit. It has linear, deep green leaves and strikingly deep blue flowers, borne profusely from mid-spring to early summer. It prefers well-drained, moist, acid soil.

Omphalodes verna
This charming spreading perennial, a relative of the forget-me-nots, grows from the south-east Alps to Romania. Its dark green, grooved leaves cover the ground and in spring, small, white-centred, deep blue flowers appear on short, branched stems, each with two to four blooms.

Tower of Jewels

Echium wildpretii

The tower of jewels is endemic to the Canary Islands. It produces a tall spike of crimson flowers with beautiful rosettes of silver leaves. Growing on mountains where it is mostly dry, cold and exposed to high ultraviolet radiation, this species shows similarities with other isolated alpine plant species, such as lobelias and groundsels, by attaining giant size to cope with alpine conditions instead of the more common miniature proportions usually associated with alpine plants. The plant is monocarpic: when the flowers fade, it dies, leaving behind a vast amount of seed.

Identification: A woody-stemmed, unbranched biennial or occasionally short-lived perennial, with a dense rosette of narrowly lance-shaped, silvery, hairy, light green leaves, to 20cm/8in long. In its first year it develops only leaves but in the following year it produces a dense, column-like cyme, 2.5m/8ft tall or more, of funnel-shaped, red or pink flowers, which are often bird-pollinated.

Distribution: Canary Islands.
Height and spread: 2–3m x 75cm/6½–10 x 2½ft.
Habit and form: Biennial.
Leaf shape: Lanceolate.
Pollinated: Bird, bee.

Above: Each flower spike is made up of a multitude of tiny, pink flowers.

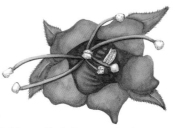

NETTLE AND DEADNETTLE FAMILIES

The nettle family, Urticaceae, is widely spread over the world. Most are herbs but a few are shrubs or small trees, mainly tropical, though several occur widely in temperate climates. Many of the species have stinging hairs on their stems and leaves. The Lamiaceae, or deadnettle family, are mostly herbs or shrubs, distributed all over the world. They include many well-known herbs, ornamental plants and weeds.

Stinging Nettle

Urtica dioica

The common stinging nettle is an upright perennial that grows in damp forests or wherever land has been disturbed by humans. It has a much-branched yellow rhizome, which spreads over large areas, and from which grow numerous leafy shoots. The unisexual flowers are borne on separate plants, although monoecious specimens sometimes occur. All parts of the plant are covered in fine, stinging hairs: it is soon recognized, often through harsh experience!

Above: Tiny female flowers appear on separate plants to male ones (left).

Identification: Numerous erect, quadrangular stems commonly grow to 1.2m/4ft tall, although they may far exceed this in favourable conditions. They are covered with long stinging hairs and short bristly hairs. The opposite, stalked, heart-shaped or lance-shaped leaves are serrated at the margin and covered on both sides with translucent stinging hairs. The flowers are arranged in drooping panicles, growing in groups from the upper leaf axils from late spring to early autumn.

Distribution: Northern Eurasia.
Height and spread: 1.2m/4ft.
Habit and form: Herbaceous perennial.
Leaf shape: Cordate or lanceolate.
Pollinated: Wind.

Left and right: These robust plants spread to form extensive colonies.

China Grass

White ramie, *Boehmeria nivea*

This shrubby perennial from eastern Asia has the overall appearance of a stinging nettle, but lacks any stinging hairs. It can sometimes be encountered in the wild in rocky places up to a height of 1,200m/4,000ft. It is often found outside its original range due to its having been extensively cultivated for its fibres, which, when extracted from the stems, are the longest and strongest of any plant. It is sometimes found wild in India, Malaysia, China and Japan, and is probably a native of India and Malaysia.

Identification: A number of straight, coarse, bristly shoots are sent up from a perennial underground rootstock each season. The alternate leaves are broadly oval, 15cm/6in long or more, with pointed tips, wedge-shaped or rounded at the base, serrated along the margin, white-woolly underneath, giving a silvery appearance. The minute, greenish flowers are closely arranged along a slender axis, on densely branched panicles, mostly shorter than the flower stalk.

Distribution: Eastern Asia.
Height and spread: 1–1.8m x 1m/3–6ft x 3ft.
Habit and form: Shrubby, herbaceous perennial.
Leaf shape: Ovate.
Pollinated: Wind.

OTHER NETTLE AND DEADNETTLES

Sage *Salvia officinalis*
Sage originates in southern Europe, growing on dry banks and in stony places, usually in limestone areas and often where there is very little soil. A small evergreen shrub, rarely exceeding 60cm/2ft, it sports scented, purple flowers from early to late summer. The whole plant is extremely aromatic, hence its long culinary use.

Pellitory of the Wall *Parietaria judaica*
This perennial, grows to 60cm/2ft, in semi-shade or an open position. It is often found on hedge banks and dry walls, hence the name. It has the reputation of being a medicinal plant, and is often found growing around ruined castles, churches and monasteries.

Water Mint *Mentha aquatica*
One of the commonest wild mints, often found around marshes, fens, near rivers, streams and ponds, and in wet woods. When crushed it imparts a characteristic rich aroma. It hybridizes easily with other mints, often crossing with spearmint, *M. spicata*, to produce peppermint, *M. x piperita*.

Roman Nettle *Urtica pilulifera*
The Roman nettle bears its female flowers in little compact, globular heads, followed by ornamental seedpods, and was a medicinal plant of choice for the ancient Romans. It is also smooth except for the stinging hairs, which contain a much more virulent venom than that of the common stinging nettle.

Aluminium Plant

Watermelon pilea, *Pilea cadierei*

This familiar plant is widely grown in gardens, or as a houseplant, although its origins are in the warm humid forests of Vietnam. It is instantly recognizable due to the variegated foliage that is unlike any other, with shiny silver, irregularly-shaped markings parallel to the lateral veins. These leaves are held opposite each other on square, green stems and they rapidly produce a thick ground cover in patches of open forest. Its small white flowers are produced at the ends of the stems in the summer but are mostly overshadowed by the conspicuous foliage.

Distribution: Vietnam.
Height and spread: 50cm/20in.
Habit and form: Spreading evergreen perennial.
Leaf shape: Oval.
Pollinated: Bee.

Identification: Spreading to erect herb or sub-shrub, to 45cm/1½ft, with greenish or pink-tinged, soft, round stems, becoming rigid with age and woody at the base. The leaves are obovate to oblong-oblanceolate to 7.5cm/3in long, held in opposite pairs, simple, quilted, green with interrupted bands of silver centrally and on margins, with coppery-maroon veins. The flowers are minute, whitish becoming pinkish, perianth with four segments in male flowers, three in female.

Below: The shiny, irregular markings on the leaves are instantly recognizable and give rise to this plant's common name.

Mind-your-own-business

Soleirolia soleirolii

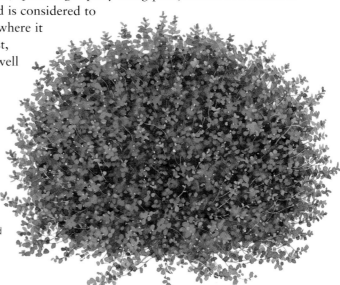

This semi-evergreen, creeping perennial, which forms a dense mat about 5cm/2in high, was originally introduced as an ornamental from Corsica across much of its modern range. It prefers moist soil and partial shade, spreading rapidly using pink, thread-like stems. It sometimes forms extensive mats and is considered to be an invasive weed in many areas where it has been introduced. It prefers moist, sheltered habitats and is especially well adapted for colonizing urban areas.

Distribution: Corsica, but now very widespread.
Height and spread: 5cm/2in, with indefinite spread.
Habit and form: Creeping herbaceous perennial.
Leaf shape: Rounded.
Pollinated: Wind.

Identification: The slender stems, which grow to 20cm/8in and root at the nodes, are delicate, intricately branching, translucent, pale green sometimes tinged pink. The leaves, 2–6mm/1⁄16–1⁄4in, are alternate and near-circular, short-stalked, minutely and sparsely hairy with a smooth margin. The solitary flowers, borne in the leaf axils, are minute, white, sometimes pink tinged, and followed by the glossy, one-seeded fruit, enclosed in a persistent calyx.

FIGWORT FAMILY

The Scrophulariaceae, or figwort family, comprise mostly herbs but also a few small shrubs, with about 190 genera and 4,000 predominately temperate species. They include many that are partial root parasites and a few that are without chlorophyll and are wholly parasitic. They have a cosmopolitan distribution, with the majority found in temperate areas, including tropical mountains.

Cape Fuchsia

Phygelius capensis

The common name of this plant reflects the flower shape, with long tubular flowers bearing a resemblance to those of the quite unrelated fuchsia. It has a very long flowering season, sometimes lasting four or five months. Originating from alongside streams in South Africa, this beautiful plant has long been cultivated for its racemes of brilliant scarlet flowers. Consequently, it is occasionally encountered as a garden escapee, usually near to habitations. It spreads extensively by root suckers and the top growth may die back to ground level if winter conditions become extremely cold.

Identification: A sprawling, stoloniferous, suckering, shrub or subshrub with lance-shaped to oval, dark green leaves up to 9cm/3½in long. They are mostly opposite in pairs, with the upper leaves sometimes alternate. In summer, it bears upright panicles, up to 60cm/2ft long, of showy, yellow-throated, scarlet-orange tubular flowers, each 5cm/2in long, with five lobes, curved back toward the stems.

Distribution: South Africa.
Height and spread: 1.2 x 2.5m/4 x 8ft.
Habit and form: Suckering subshrub.
Leaf shape: Lanceolate to ovate.
Pollinated: Insect, bird.

Left and far left: The showy, yellow-throated flowers, shaped rather like the unrelated Fuchsia *genus, appear in upright panicles during the summer and give rise to the plant's common name.*

Foxglove

Digitalis purpurea

A common biennial or occasionally short-lived perennial of woodlands, hedge banks and wayside, wherever soil is disturbed, the foxglove provides a colourful display in midsummer. The flowers are most commonly purple but can be white and occasionally pale pink. It seeds profusely: a single plant can produce up to two million seeds. It does best in sandy, well-drained areas. It is distributed throughout Europe, though is absent from some calcareous districts.

Identification: Rosette-forming and very variable, the foxglove has oval to lance-shaped, usually toothed, sometimes white, woolly, dark green leaves, 10–25cm/4–10in long. Tall stems with alternate leaves support one-sided spikes of purple, pink or white, inflated, tubular, bell-shaped, two-lipped flowers, to 6cm/2¼in long, spotted maroon to purple inside, and produced in early summer. Oval fruits, longer than the tube formed by the sepals, ripen to brown.

Top: Each flowerhead is composed of single flowers.

Distribution: Europe.
Height and spread: 1–2m x 60cm/3–6½ x 2ft.
Habit and form: Herbaceous biennial.
Leaf shape: Ovate to lanceolate.
Pollinated: Insect, chiefly bumblebee.

Left: The whole plant, including the roots and flowers, is poisonous.

Chinese Foxglove

Rehmannia glutinosa

This perennial plant from northern China is found in woodlands and stony sites and sports large, foxglove-like flowers. The species name *glutinosa* is derived from the word glutinous, referring to the sticky nature of the root. The plant received its generic name in honour of Joseph Rehmann, a 19th-century physician in the Russian city of St Petersburg. This possibly alludes to the fact that *Rehmannia*'s root is used medicinally in China, where it has been cultivated for more than 2,000 years.

Identification: This sticky, purple-hairy perennial has slender runners and rosettes of egg-shaped, scalloped, conspicuously veined, basal leaves, up to 10cm/4in long, which are mid-green above and often red tinted beneath. From mid-spring to summer, branched, leafy stems bear pendent, tubular, two-lipped flowers up to 5cm/2in long, in cyme-like racemes of a few flowers, or singly on long flower stalks, from the leaf axils. The flowers have reddish-brown tubes, marked with darker reddish-purple veins, and pale yellow-brown lips.

Distribution: Northern China.
Height and spread: 15–30cm/6–12in.
Habit and form: Herbaceous perennial.
Leaf shape: Obovate.
Pollinated: Insect, especially bee.

Far right: Large, attractive, foxglove-like flowers emerge from the middle of the leaf rosette in the spring and summer.

OTHER FIGWORT FAMILY SPECIES

Dark Mullein *Verbascum nigrum*
The dark mullein is a widely distributed plant, found all over Europe and in temperate Asia as far as the Himalayas. In the eastern states of North America it is abundant as a naturalized weed. Its yellow flower spike, up to 1.2m/4ft tall, rises from a basal rosette of soft, felted leaves in summer.

Snapdragon *Antirrhinum majus*
The snapdragon is a native of south-west Europe that has naturalized across the world, and thrives on old walls and chalk cliffs, having escaped from gardens during a long period of cultivation. Its botanical name, *Antirrhinum*, refers to the snout-like form of the flower.

Toadflax *Linaria vulgaris*
In most parts of Europe toadflax grows wild on dry banks, by the wayside, and at the borders of fields and meadows. It is especially abundant in gravelly soil and in limestone districts. It has grey-green, narrow leaves and yellow, snapdragon-like flowers on a spike up to 75cm/30in tall from midsummer to mid-autumn.

Germander Speedwell *Veronica chamaedrys*
Commonly found on banks, in pastures and woods, germander speedwell flowers in spring and early summer. It has a creeping, branched rootstock, and strong stems that sport bright blue flowers streaked with darker lines and a white eye in the centre. The flower closes at night and also in rainy weather.

Knotted Figwort

Common figwort, *Scrophularia nodosa*

The knotted figwort, common throughout western Europe, is similar in general habit to the water figwort, *S. auriculata*, though it is not distinctly an aquatic like that species. It is frequently found in woodland glades, hedge banks and in damp shady places with fairly rich soil, either in cultivated or waste ground. The "fig" in its name is an old English word for haemorrhoids, which both the globular red flowers and the root protuberances were thought to resemble.

Identification: It is an upright perennial, hairless except for the glandular inflorescence. Short rhizomes, which are irregularly tuberous, give rise to sharply four-angled, non-winged stems, which support a panicle of flower clusters growing from the axils of the bracts. The lowest bracts are leaf-like, and the flowers are two-lipped, yellowish-green, up to 12mm/½in long, each with a brown upper lip. The leaves are oval, pointed and coarsely toothed, and often unequally decurrent down the leaf stalk.

Right: The tall flower stems emerge during late spring and early summer.

Distribution: Europe.
Height and spread: 40–80cm/16–32in.
Habit and form: Herbaceous perennial.
Leaf shape: Ovate.
Pollinated: Wasp (chiefly) and bee.

Left: The individual flowers are small and yellowish-green with a brown upper lip.

ACANTHUS FAMILY

The Acanthaceae, or acanthus family, are mostly herbs or shrubs comprising about 250 genera and 2,500 species. Most are tropical herbs, shrubs or twining vines, while others are spiny. Only a few species are distributed in temperate regions. Typically, there is a colourful bract subtending each flower; in some species the bract is large and showy. The family is closely allied to the Scrophulariaceae (figworts).

Bear's Breeches

Acanthus mollis

This plant is a native of warmer parts of south-western Europe as far as the Balkans, and parts of North Africa. It is most commonly found in woodland scrub and on stony hillsides. In summer, creamy-white to slightly pink or purplish flowers appear on tall, erect stalks above the foliage. The generic name derives from the Greek *akantha*, meaning "spine", referring to the toothed foliage of some species.

Identification: This large, clump-forming perennial has oval, deeply cut, smooth, bright green foliage. The basal leaves are 20–60cm/8–24in long on long leaf stalks; those on the upper stem are 1–3cm/½–1¼in long, more or less oval, toothed and stalkless. The leaves can be quite variable, being cut, lobed, or even deeply pinnately divided. The irregular and unusual flowers form on stiff, erect spikes, well above the foliage from early to late summer. The flower is tubular, with a large, three-lobed lower lip. It is suspended by spine-tipped bracts and a large calyx lobe; another enlarged calyx lobe forms a hood.

Left: The large, spiny leaves form a dense clump from which the flower spikes emerge.

Left: Each flower spike contains many small white flowers.

Distribution: Southern Europe, north-west Africa.
Height and spread: 120 x 60cm/4 x 2ft.
Habit and form: Herbaceous perennial.
Leaf shape: Ovate.
Pollinated: Bee.

Persian Shield

Strobilanthes dyerianus

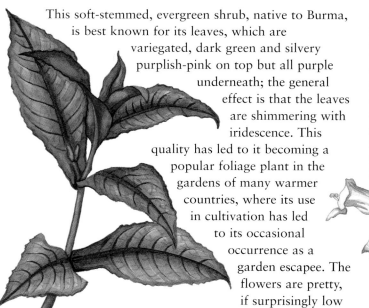

This soft-stemmed, evergreen shrub, native to Burma, is best known for its leaves, which are variegated, dark green and silvery purplish-pink on top but all purple underneath; the general effect is that the leaves are shimmering with iridescence. This quality has led to it becoming a popular foliage plant in the gardens of many warmer countries, where its use in cultivation has led to its occasional occurrence as a garden escapee. The flowers are pretty, if surprisingly low key given the spectacular foliage, being funnel-shaped, pale violet, and arranged on short spikes.

Identification: An evergreen subshrub with soft (not woody) stems, square in cross section. The unequal pairs of elliptic, toothed, dark green, opposite leaves, 10–18cm/4–7in long, have a puckered texture and are variegated dark green and silvery-metallic, purplish-pink on top and all purple underneath. It bears short spikes of funnel-shaped, pale blue flowers, 3cm/1¼in long.

Left: The pretty, violet flowers appear on short spikes.

Right: Although the plant adopts a shrubby character, the stems remain quite soft and brittle.

Distribution: Burma.
Height and spread: 120 x 90cm/4 x 3ft.
Habit and form: Evergreen subshrub.
Leaf shape: Elliptic.
Pollinated: Insect.

OTHER ACANTHUS FAMILY SPECIES

Acanthus spinosus
Much like its relative *A. mollis*, this herbaceous plant from west Turkey grows about 1m/3ft tall, but its leaves are more spiny and narrower. In summer, white flowers wrapped in pretty, spiny, mauve-purple bracts are borne on tall, erect stalks above the foliage.

Firecracker Flower *Crossandra infundibuliformis*
The firecracker flower is a tropical shrub, native to southern India and Sri Lanka. Fan-shaped flowers appear in clusters on long stems, growing from the leaf axils. The flowers are yellow or salmon-orange in colour and can bloom continuously for weeks.

Bengal Clock Vine
Thunbergia grandiflora
The Bengal clock vine, or blue trumpet vine, is a vigorous, woody-stemmed climber from northern India, with broad-lobed leaves, bearing pendent racemes of large, showy violet or whitish flowers, with pale yellow tubes, which may reach 4cm/1½in long and 7.5cm/3in across.

Acanthus hungaricus
A large, evergreen, clump-forming, herbaceous perennial from the Balkans, Romania and Greece, with long, handsome, shiny, deeply cut, thistle-like, basal leaves. Tall spikes of white or pink-flushed flowers with red-purple bracts emerge in early to midsummer.

Black-eyed Susan

Thunbergia alata

This familiar climbing plant, usually grown in cultivation as an annual, is actually an evergreen perennial in tropical climates. It is often found outside its natural range as a garden escapee. It is a fast-growing climber, native to tropical areas of east Africa, which twines around any convenient support, and bears bright orange flowers with black centres throughout summer. The genus name honours Carl Peter Thunberg, an 18th-century Swedish botanist.

Identification: This tropical evergreen twining vine, climbing or trailing, has triangular to egg-shaped leaves, sharply pointed, shaped like an arrowhead at the base, up to 7.5cm/3in long, entire or with a few coarse teeth; the leaf stalks are winged, about as long as the leaf. Solitary, flat, five-petalled, orange-yellow flowers, rarely white, to 5cm/2in wide, with black-purple flower tubes, are borne from the leaf axils on stalks longer than the leaf stalks. The flattened round seed capsule is about 12mm/½in wide, with a beak 12mm/½in long; the seeds are warty and ribbed.

Left: A vigorous climbing habit and free-flowering nature have made this plant popular in cultivation.

Distribution: Tropical east Africa.
Height and spread: 6 x 1.8m/20 x 6ft.
Habit and form: Evergreen climbing perennial.
Leaf shape: Deltoid or ovate.
Pollinated: Insect.

Above left: The stems are twining.

Adhatoda

Malabar nut tree, Adulsa, Vasaka, *Justicia adhatoda*

Adhatoda is common in India, especially in the lower Himalayas (up to 1,300m/4,250ft above sea level) and to a slightly lesser extent in Sri Lanka. It favours open plains and is commonly found growing on wasteland. It is a small tree or large shrub that flowers in the cold season. Adhatoda leaves have been used extensively in Ayurvedic medicine for more than 2,000 years.

Identification: Adhatoda has smooth, ash-coloured bark, which is smoother on the branches. The opposite, broadly lance-shaped, taper-pointed, smooth or slightly downy leaves, which are 12.5–15cm/5–6in long, are borne on short leaf stalks. The solitary flower spikes emerge from the exterior axils on long stalks, the whole end of the branchlet forming a leafy panicle enveloped with large bracts. The white, tubular flowers are spotted with small rust-coloured dots; the lower part of both lips is streaked with purple. The fruit is a small, four-seeded capsule.

Distribution: Indian subcontinent.
Height and spread: 3 x 1.5m/10 x 5ft.
Habit and form: Evergreen shrub.
Leaf shape: Broadly lanceolate.
Pollinated: Insect.

Far right: Adhatoda is a usually erect and sparsely branched evergreen shrub, spreading with age.

Below: The rust-speckled white flowers are streaked with purple.

DAISY FAMILY

The Asteraceae, or daisy family, are herbaceous plants, shrubs or, less commonly, trees. This is arguably the largest family of flowering plants, comprising about 1,100 genera and 20,000 species. The species are characterized by having the flowers reduced and organized into a composite arrangement of tiny individual flowers called a capitulum – a tight cluster that superficially resembles a single bloom.

Daisy

Bellis perennis

Arguably the most widely recognized of all wild flowers, the daisy grows on roadsides, in gardens, and is often an unwanted weed. The plant is most commonly found growing in short grassland, particularly in cultivated lawns. It requires moist soil and the seeds usually germinate on worm casts left on the surface.

Identification: A stoloniferous, evergreen, rosette-forming perennial, with a flat basal rosette of spoon-shaped, bright green leaves, 1.2–6cm/½–2½in long. From late winter to late summer, slightly hairy stems, 2.5–10cm/1–4in tall, carry single, large, white compound flowers, 1.2–3cm/½–1¼in across, with white ray florets, often tinged maroon or pink, and yellow disc florets, from pink buds.

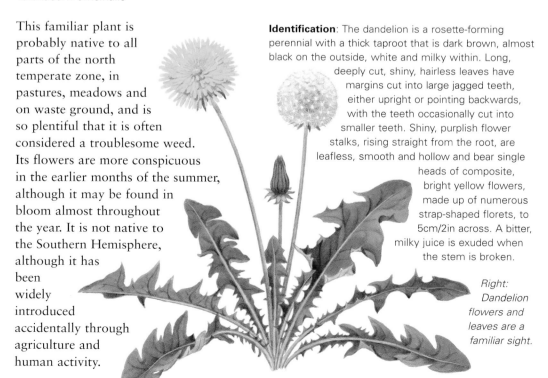

Below: Daisy flowers open outright in full sun.

Distribution: Europe and Turkey.
Height and spread: 15cm/6in.
Habit and form: Evergreen perennial.
Leaf shape: Obovate.
Pollinated: Bee, fly and beetle.

Dandelion

Taraxacum officinalis

This familiar plant is probably native to all parts of the north temperate zone, in pastures, meadows and on waste ground, and is so plentiful that it is often considered a troublesome weed. Its flowers are more conspicuous in the earlier months of the summer, although it may be found in bloom almost throughout the year. It is not native to the Southern Hemisphere, although it has been widely introduced accidentally through agriculture and human activity.

Identification: The dandelion is a rosette-forming perennial with a thick taproot that is dark brown, almost black on the outside, white and milky within. Long, deeply cut, shiny, hairless leaves have margins cut into large jagged teeth, either upright or pointing backwards, with the teeth occasionally cut into smaller teeth. Shiny, purplish flower stalks, rising straight from the root, are leafless, smooth and hollow and bear single heads of composite, bright yellow flowers, made up of numerous strap-shaped florets, to 5cm/2in across. A bitter, milky juice is exuded when the stem is broken.

Right: Dandelion flowers and leaves are a familiar sight.

Distribution: Worldwide in temperate regions, often introduced elsewhere.
Height and spread: Up to 30cm/1ft.
Habit and form: Herbaceous perennial.
Leaf shape: Runcinate.
Pollinated: Insect, especially bumblebee.

Sweet Coltsfoot

Giant butterbur, Japanese butterbur, fuki, *Petasites japonicus*

Distribution: East Asia: China, Japan and Korea.
Height and spread: 60 × 150cm/2–3ft.
Habit and form: Herbaceous perennial.
Leaf shape: Reniform.
Pollinated: Insect.

Far right: The large leaves appearing in summer offer stark contrast to the small bracts of the flower stems.

This species is a native of eastern Asia, naturally inhabiting damp, marshy areas, especially along riverbanks, although it is widely naturalized elsewhere as a garden escapee in moist woods and thickets. The plant is a master of metamorphosis, as it changes from an unimposing small flower stalk to a mound of large, kidney-shaped leaves on long, edible stalks. Individual plants are either male or female and both sexes must be present if seed is to be set. It can form very large colonies where conditions are favourable for its growth. The name "butterbur" comes from a related European species reportedly used to wrap butter, despite the unpleasant smell.

Identification: Growing from a rhizome, the plant has kidney-shaped, irregularly toothed, basal leaves up to 80cm/32in across, hairy beneath, borne on stalks 90cm/3ft long. Densely clustered corymbs of yellowish-white flowerheads, to 1.5cm/⅝in across, with oblong bracts below, are borne before the leaves in late winter and early spring.

OTHER DAISY FAMILY SPECIES

Leopard Plant *Ligularia przewalskii*
A native of northern China, this clump-forming perennial has huge, heart-shaped, leathery, deeply cut, toothed, dark green leaves that emerge purplish-red, but turn to brownish-green. Tall, narrow spikes of clear yellow, daisy-like flowers appear from mid- to late summer.

Globe Thistle *Echinops ritro*
A native from central Europe to central Asia, growing to 50cm/20in or more. The stiff, spiny leaves are dark green and "cobwebby" above and white-downy below. In summer it bears spherical flowerheads, up to 5cm/2in across, which change from metallic blue to bright blue as the florets open.

Ox-eye Daisy *Leucanthemum vulgare*

A familiar sight in fields throughout Europe and northern Asia. The generic name, derived from Greek means "white flower". The familiar yellow-centred, white flowerheads appear from late spring until midsummer.

Cornflower *Centaurea cyanus*
The cornflower, with its star-like blossoms of brilliant blue, is a most striking wildflower. It is fairly common in cultivated fields and by roadsides, though is in decline due to changing agricultural practices. The down-covered stems are tough and wiry.

Namaqualand Daisy

Dimorphotheca sinuata

This showy annual grows naturally in the winter rainfall areas of south-western Africa, usually in sandy places in Namaqualand and Namibia. It creates sheets of brilliant orange when it flowers in early spring, drawing visitors from near and far. The genus name is derived from Greek *dis* (twice), *morphe* (shape) and *theka* (fruit), referring to the different kinds of seeds produced by the ray and disc flowers.

Identification: The aromatic leaves are slender, oblong to lance-shaped, or sometimes spoon-shaped, with coarsely toothed margins, light green, up to 10cm/4in long. The stems are reddish and covered by the masses of leaves around them. The orange, or occasionally white to yellow flowers, up to 8cm/3¼in across, borne singly at the tip of each stem in winter, have orange centres (sometimes yellow). They need full sun to open and always face the sun. Around the centre at the bottom of the petals is a narrow, greenish-mauve ring.

Left: The brilliant orange, tall-stemmed daisy-like flowers grow out of a mat of foliage.

Distribution: South-west Africa.
Height and spread: 30cm/1ft.
Habit and form: Annual.
Leaf shape: Oblong to lanceolate or obovate.
Pollinated: Insect.

ERICACEOUS PLANTS

The Ericaceae are a large family, mostly shrubby in character, comprising about 125 genera and 3,500 species of mostly calcifuge (lime-hating) plants, generally restricted to acid soils. The family is cosmopolitan in distribution, except in deserts, and includes numerous plants from temperate, boreal and montane tropical zones. The chief centre of diversity is in southern Africa.

Scarlet Heath

Erica coccinea

A rather variable species of heather, the scarlet heath is commonly found in the fynbos vegetation of the south-west Cape in South Africa, although it is most often noticed during its peak flowering season. This is mainly during the wetter, winter months but it can be variable depending upon the form. As with many of the long-flowered heathers, this species is typically pollinated by small birds or more occasionally insects and has long tubular flowers that reflect this relationship.

Identification: An erect, much-branched evergreen shrub with numerous short, lateral, leafy branchlets, tightly clustered along the main branches. They are covered in small, needle-like leaves, 4–8mm/⅛–⅜in long, arranged in whorls of three. Both leafy and flowering growth is mainly hairless. Pendent, showy flowers, growing from just below the branch end are 6–15mm/¼–⅝in long, in a range of colours from red, pink and orange, to yellow or green.

Distribution: South Africa.
Height and spread: 1.2m/4ft.
Habit and form: Evergreen shrub.
Leaf shape: Linear.
Pollinated: Bird, occasionally insect.

Above left: The long tubular flowers of this species of heather are often pollinated by small birds.

Rhododendron ponticum

A fast-growing, evergreen, small tree or large shrub, which occurs naturally in three main regions: around the Black Sea, in the Balkans and in the Iberian Peninsula. It can grow up to 6m/20ft in favoured conditions, which are, generally, acidic moorland and woodland. However, it is happy in almost any conditions, from open sunny spots to quite dense shade, and has become an invasive pest in Britain and other European countries. Fossil evidence in Irish peat deposits reveals that this plant once occurred as a native there, approximately 302,000–428,000 years ago, in a warm period that interrupted the most recent ice age, suggesting that it was once far more widespread than it is currently.

Identification: This vigorous, evergreen shrub has inversely lance-shaped to broadly elliptic, leathery leaves, 6–18cm/2¼–7in long, glossy, dark green above and paler beneath. In early summer it bears trusses of broadly funnel-shaped, reddish-purple, mauve or occasionally white flowers, up to 5cm/2in long, often spotted yellowish-green inside.

Distribution: Europe and Western Asia.
Height and spread: 6m/20ft.
Habit and form: Evergreen shrub.
Leaf shape: Broadly elliptic.
Pollinated: Insect, especially bee.

Left: The tightly arranged flowerheads appear in mid-spring.

Right: Rhododendron ponticum can form a large bush in time and often forms dense stands in light woodland cover.

Bearberry

Arctostaphylos uva-ursi

Distribution: Circumpolar.
Height and spread:
30cm/1ft.
Habit and form: Trailing
evergreen shrub.
Leaf shape: Obovate.
Pollinated: Insect.

The bearberry is a small shrub, distributed over the greater part of the Northern Hemisphere, being found in the northern latitudes and high mountains of Europe, Asia and North America, throughout Canada and the United States. It is common on heaths and barren places in hilly districts.

Identification: A much-branched, evergreen shrub, it has irregular, short, woody stems covered with a pale brown bark, scaling off in patches, which trail along the ground forming thick masses, 30–60cm/1–2ft in length. Evergreen, leathery leaves, 12–25mm/½–1in long, are spoon-shaped, tapering gradually towards the base to a very short stalk, with entire, slightly rolled back margins. The upper leaf surface is shiny dark green with deeply impressed veins; the underside is paler, with prominent veins forming a coarse network. The young leaves are fringed with short hairs. Small, waxy-looking, urn-shaped flowers, reddish-white or white with a red lip, transparent at the base, contracted at the mouth, in small, crowded, drooping clusters, appear at the ends of the branches in early summer, before the young leaves.

Far left: The evergreen, branching growth often forms a dense mass that hugs the ground.

Left: The small flowers appear on the branch tips in early summer. The leaves are simple.

OTHER ERICACEOUS PLANT SPECIES

Bilberry *Vaccinium myrtillus*
The bilberry, or whinberry, is a small, branched shrub of heaths and mountainous areas, with wiry angular branches, bearing globular waxy flowers and edible black berries, which are covered with a delicate grey bloom when ripe. The leathery leaves are at first rosy, then yellowish-green, turning red in autumn.

Heather *Calluna vulgaris*
Heather, or ling, is an abundant, sometimes dominant plant over large areas of heath and moorland, particularly along the Atlantic fringe of Europe. An evergreen shrub growing to 60cm/2ft, it sports a profusion of small, bell-shaped, pink flowers in late summer.

Marsh Andromeda
Andromeda polifolia
Known as bog rosemary, this subshrub chiefly occurs on raised bogs in northern Eurasia and the USA. The flowers are small, spherical, pink and produced in spring and early summer. The plant is threatened by the destruction of its habitat.

Enkianthus campanulatus
This deciduous, bushy, spreading, tree-like shrub from Japan has an upright, narrow, layered branch habit and red shoots with tufts of dull green leaves that turn bright red in autumn. In spring, large terminal flower buds open to reveal small, bell-shaped, red-veined, creamy-yellow flowers.

Rhododendron ambiguum

Rhododendrons are a hugely diverse genus, with their centre of diversity occurring in Asia, especially in the east. This attractive, yellow-flowered rhododendron is native to near Mount Omei and Kangding in west Sichuan, China, where it grows in thickets on wooded hillsides and rocky, exposed slopes from 1,800–3,000m/5,900–9,850ft.

Identification: On this upright but compact, evergreen shrub, the bark of mature shoots is usually smooth, red-brown and peeling. The leaves are narrowly oval to elliptic, up to 7.5cm/3in long, shiny dark green above and blue-green beneath with a strong midrib. Loose trusses of between three and five widely funnel-shaped flowers, to 4cm/1½in, arise from terminal inflorescences in mid-spring. They are pale to greenish-yellow, often with greenish spots on the upper lobe, and with lobes as long as the tube.

Distribution: Sichuan and Guizhou, China.
Height and spread: 2m/6½ft or more.
Habit and form: Evergreen shrub.
Leaf shape: Ovate.
Pollinated: Bee.

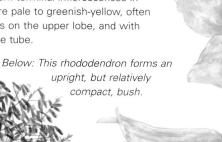

Below: This rhododendron forms an upright, but relatively compact, bush.

Left: The attractive trusses of funnel-shaped, pale greenish-yellow flowers appear in spring.

NIGHTSHADE AND BINDWEED FAMILIES

The Solanaceae, or nightshade family, are herbaceous perennials, shrubs, or trees of about 85 genera and 2,800 species. They are frequently vines or creepers, and while some are edible, others are considered very poisonous. The bindweed family are twining herbs or shrubs, sometimes with milky sap, comprise 1,500 species. Many have heart-shaped leaves and funnel-shaped solitary or paired flowers.

Henbane

Hyoscyamus niger

A widespread, but infrequent annual or biennial, henbane is found throughout central and southern Europe to India and Siberia, often occurring on waste ground, near buildings and in stony places from low-lying ground near the sea to lower mountain slopes. As a weed of cultivation it now also grows in North America and Brazil. It is poisonous in all its parts, and is the source of the chemical hyoscine, used medicinally as a sedative.

Identification: A variable, coarse, leafy, branched, strong-scented plant, henbane is conspicuously sticky and hairy, especially the stout stem. The stalkless leaves are alternate and numerous, often on one side of the branches. They are oval to broadly lance-shaped, 5–20cm/2–8in long, rather shallowly pinnately lobed, with up to ten unequal, triangular, pointed segments. Numerous funnel-shaped flowers appear between late spring and late summer, in one-sided rows on long, downward-curving branches. The flowers are 2.5–5cm/1–2in long and nearly or quite as wide at the top, prominently purple-veined on a pale, often greenish-yellow background, more distinctly purple in the throat.

Below: The fruit capsules contain up to 500 seeds.

Below: Henbane is woody.

Right: The five rounded lobes of the flowerheads are slightly unequal.

Distribution: Eurasia.
Height and spread: 90cm/3ft.
Habit and form: Annual or biennial.
Leaf shape: Ovate.
Pollinated: Insect.

Chinese Lantern

Winter cherry, *Physalis alkekengi*

Chinese lantern is a widespread species, found from Central Europe to China. The name *Physalis* is from the Greek *phusa* (bladder), referring to the bladder-like calyx enclosing the fruit. The shape of the calyx also accounts for the plant's common name. The berries are edible and very juicy, if acrid and bitter; all other parts of the plant, except the ripe fruit, are poisonous. The calyx and skin of the fruit include a yellow colouring matter that has been used for butter.

Left: The tall stems arise each season from underground rhizomes.

Far right: The creamy flowers give rise to the showy "lanterns".

Identification: This vigorous, spreading, rhizomatous perennial has triangular-oval to diamond-shaped leaves, up to 12.5cm/5in long. Nodding, bell-shaped, cream flowers, 2cm/¾in long, with star-shaped mouths, are produced from the leaf axils in midsummer. They are followed by large, bright orange-scarlet berries, enclosed in five-sided, papery, red calyces, that greatly increase in size by the autumn to form large, leafy bladders up to 5cm/2in across.

Distribution: Caucasus to China.
Height and spread: 30 x 60cm/1–2ft.
Habit and form: Herbaceous perennial.
Leaf shape: Triangular-ovate.
Pollinated: Bee.

Giant Bindweed

Calystegia silvatica

Distribution: Eurasia and North America.
Height and spread: Up to 5m/16ft.
Habit and form: Herbaceous climber.
Leaf shape: Cordate or sagittate.
Pollinated: Insect.

Bindweeds are known as "morning glories", referring to their habit of opening early in the day, with the bloom fading by mid-afternoon. Giant bindweed has alternate leaves, and is characterized by showy, white, funnel-shaped flowers, usually appearing in spring until early autumn. The plant is very widespread, with subspecies occurring across Eurasia and North America. The genus *Calystegia* can be distinguished from the closely related *Convolvulus* genus by its floral characteristics: *Calystegia* species have a pair of large bracts that overlap the calyx, whereas *Convolvulus* species have very small bracts that are distant from the calyx.

Above: The tightly wrapped buds unfurl in the morning, but each flower lasts just one day.

Left: Despite its showy flowers, its vigorous smothering habit have made this plant unpopular in cultivated areas.

Identification: A strong, rampant, stoloniferous, perennial climber, with stems up to 5m/16ft and alternate, heart-shaped or arrowhead-shaped leaves, up to 15cm/6in long. White, rarely pink-striped, trumpet-shaped flowers are between 6–9cm/2¼–3½in across, rarely deeply five-lobed, with bracts strongly pouched and overlapping. It may be confused with the related *C. sepium*, although its has larger flowers than that species.

OTHER NIGHTSHADE AND BINDWEED SPECIES

Mandrake
Mandragora officinarum
The mandrake, the object of strange superstitions, is native to southern Europe. Its large brown, parsnip-like root runs deep into the ground. Dark green leaves spread open and lie upon the ground, among which primrose-like white, purplish or bluish flowers appear in summer or autumn, followed by yellow fruits.

Convolvulus tricolor
This annual or short-lived perennial grows up to around 60cm/2ft and has large, trumpet-shaped, sky-blue to dark blue flowers, with white-and-yellow throats, during the summer. Native to the Mediterranean region, the plant is present as a garden escapee in many other regions.

Yellow Henbane *Hyoscyamus aureus*
A biennial or occasionally perennial plant with an erect but brittle habit. It has fairly large yellow flowers that are tinged purple toward the centre. It is a common sight in old walls, dry soils and shingle, especially around the Mediterranean.

Mallow-leaved Bindweed
Convolvulus althaeoides
A low-growing, trailing perennial that produces rosy-pink or pink to purple, funnel-shaped flowers over silvery to grey-green leaves in early to midsummer. It is common on dry rocky soils in the Mediterranean and southern Europe.

Black Nightshade

Solanum nigrum

The black nightshade is an annual, one of the most common and cosmopolitan of wild plants, extending almost over the whole globe. It is frequently seen by the wayside and is often found on rubbish heaps, but also among growing crops and in damp and shady places. It is sometimes called the garden nightshade, because it so often occurs in cultivated ground. The berries contain the alkaloid solanine, which is toxic, and may be fatal if ingested in large quantities. The plant flowers and fruits freely, and in the autumn the masses of black berries are very noticeable.

Identification: A variable, hairy, much branched, annual herb. The stem is green and hollow, up to 30cm/1ft in height. Oval to lance-shaped leaves have bluntly notched or waved margins, usually untoothed. The flowers are white, with yellow anthers, approximately 6mm/¼in, in clusters of about five at the ends of stalks. The berry-like fruits are green at first and dull black when ripe.

Distribution: Worldwide.
Height and spread: Up to 30cm/1ft.
Habit and form: Annual.
Leaf shape: Ovate to lanceolate.
Pollinated: Insect.

Above: The berries turn from green to black from late summer onward.

Far left: Vigorous and free branching, black nightshade becomes a bushy mass.

DOGWOOD AND PROTEA FAMILIES

The Cornaceae, or dogwoods, are woody shrubs and trees found mostly in the northern temperate zone. The Proteaceae, or proteas, include about 80 genera and 1,500 species, with representatives in South America, South Africa, India, Australia and New Zealand. The name is derived from the shape-shifting Greek god Proteus, in reference to the extreme variability of leaf form in the family.

Swedish Cornel

Cornus suecica

Swedish cornel forms lovely colourful patches among dwarf shrubs in heaths, open thickets and forests in northern regions. The flowerheads are extremely showy consisting of four large white bracts, surrounding small purple flowers, which appear mainly in early summer. These are followed later in the year by small bunches of bright red fruit. The plant is widely distributed in northen Europe to north Japan, and in northern North America. The flowers are quite unusual in that they open "explosively", possibly to help spread pollen if there are too few insects around.

Identification: *Cornus suecica* is a low-growing, rhizomatous perennial, with slender, freely branching creeping stems emanating from a woody underground rootstock. A few opposite pairs of stem leaves, and egg-shaped to lance-shaped, mid-green leaves in terminal whorls are borne on short stems. In early summer, inconspicuous, purple-red flowers are surrounded by four white, 12mm/½in long, elliptic bracts, in a cyme 2.5cm/1in across. They are followed by clusters of scarlet fruits. The foliage gradually changes to bright red in the autumn.

Distribution: Circumboreal.
Height and spread: 10–15 x 30cm/4–6 x 12in.
Habit and form: Creeping herbaceous perennial.
Leaf shape: Ovate to lanceolate.
Pollinated: Insect.

Left: The berries are bright red and appear in profusion on the shrub in the autumn.

Tatarian Dogwood

Red-barked dogwood, *Cornus alba*

This suckering, deciduous, colonizing shrub, found throughout Siberia to Manchuria and northern Korea, forms clumps of stems reaching a height of up to 3m/10ft. The young twigs are an intense blood-red in the winter and the leaves turn many beautiful colours. The insignificant flower cymes are followed by white to very pale blue fruits.

Identification: Most stems of this upright shrub branch little, except near the tip. It has vivid blood-red bark in winter, which in spring reverts to nearly green. It is smooth, except for lenticels, or leaf scars, which encircle the stems. The leaves are opposite, simple, oval to elliptic, tapering to a point, 5–11.5cm/2–4½in long, with the major leaf veins parallel to the curving leaf margins. They emerge yellow-green, darkening with maturity to medium or dark green and often reddening in autumn. Small, yellowish-white flowers are held in flattened cymes, 4–5cm/ 1½–2in in diameter, in late spring to early summer. The fruits, white or tinged blue, ripen in midsummer.

Distribution: North Asia.
Height and spread: 3m/10ft.
Habit and form: Deciduous shrub.
Leaf shape: Ovate to elliptic.
Pollinated: Insect.

Left: The berries.

Right: Cornus is often cultivated as a garden plant, or planted on banks at the side of busy roads for its winter foliage. The stems of the shrub turn deep pink or orange and remain that colour throughout the autumn and winter.

OTHER DOGWOOD AND PROTEA SPECIES

Cornus mas

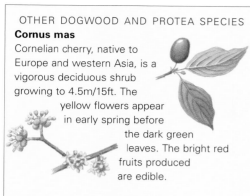

Cornelian cherry, native to Europe and western Asia, is a vigorous deciduous shrub growing to 4.5m/15ft. The yellow flowers appear in early spring before the dark green leaves. The bright red fruits produced are edible.

Protea neriifolia

Protea neriifolia has the distinction of being the first *Protea* ever to be mentioned in botanical literature. It is a very widespread species and occurs from sea-level to 4265ft/1300m altitude in the southern coastal mountain ranges from just east of Cape Town to Port Elizabeth, South Africa.

Leucadendron argenteum

This beautiful tree with its soft silver leaves is in nature almost endemic to Table Mountain and particularly to the slopes above Kirstenbosch Botanical Gardens, South Africa, where it grows in dense stands. The grey-green leaves are covered with fine, silvery hairs, which reflect the light and give the leaves a soft, velvet feel.

Peninsula Conebush *Leucadendron strobilinum*
This stout shrub is endemic to the Cape Penninsula, and is most abundant at higher altitudes and to the north, being especially common on Table Mountain. It has separate male and female plants, which grows in damp rocky situations.

King Protea

Protea cynaroides

Probably the best-known protea, this plant is prized worldwide as a magnificent cut flower and in South Africa is honoured as the national flower. The king protea has one of the widest distribution ranges of the genus, occurring across the south-west coast of South Africa, except for the dry interior ranges, at all elevations from sea level to 1,500m/4,900ft. Large, vigorous plants produce six to ten flowerheads in one season, although some exceptional plants can produce up to 40 on one plant.

Identification: The king protea is a woody shrub with thick stems. Its height and spread may vary according to locality and habitat, but all plants have large, dark green, rounded to elliptic, glossy leaves. Goblet or bowl-shaped flowerheads, 12.5–30cm/ 5–12in in diameter, are surrounded by large, colourful bracts, from creamy-white to deep crimson, produced at various times of the year according to location.

Left: Each flowerhead, is 30cm/12in diameter.

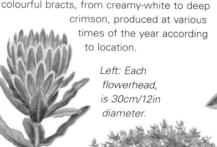

Right: King protea is a low-growing bush.

Distribution: South Africa.
Height and spread: 90cm–2m/3–6½ft.
Habit and form: Evergreen shrub.
Leaf shape: Rounded to elliptic.
Pollinated: Bird.

Yellow Pincushion

Leucospermum conocarpodendron

This species falls into the category of "tree pincushions" because it has a single, thick trunk. It is locally abundant throughout the granite and sandstone soils on dry slopes in the northern Cape Peninsula of South Africa. The flowers are bright golden-yellow and the bush is quite spectacular when it is covered in an abundance of flowers. Flowering usually commences as soon as the hot weather starts. The fruit is released two months after flowering and is dispersed by ants.

Distribution: Northern Cape Peninsula, South Africa.
Height and spread: 5 x 3m/16 x 10ft.
Habit and form: Rounded shrub.
Leaf shape: Lanceolate to elliptic.
Pollinated: Bird.

Identification: Though it is a large shrub it has a rounded, compact, neat appearance. Large lance-shaped to elliptic, stalked, grey-silver leaves, covered with a layer of minute hairs, toothed at the end and tipped with red dots, are crowded around the upright stems. The flowers, about 8cm/3¼in in diameter, are like large pincushions, with numerous bright lemon-yellow, white-tipped segments.

Left: The shrub is laden with flowers in early summer, and they are visited by pollinating birds.

MILKWEEDS AND GESNERIADS

The Asclepiadaceae, or milkweeds, are mostly herbaceous perennials and shrubs with white (often poisonous) sap comprising about 250 genera and 2,000 species, many of which are vines and some of which are cactus-like succulents with reduced leaves. The Gesneriaceae (gesneriads) are herbs, shrubs, or rarely trees and include 133 genera and 3,000 species, including many well-known ornamental species.

Silk Vine

Periploca graeca

The generic name for this vine comes from the Greek *peri* (around) and *ploke* (woven), and refers to its twining habit. The glossy leaves provide a perfect foil for the interesting, if unpleasantly scented, star-shaped flowers, which are followed by curious fruits. The silk vine is usually found in woods, thickets and riverbanks throughout this range. All parts of the plant emit a milky sap when broken or cut. The sap and fruit are poisonous.

Below: The flowerhead.

Identification: The silk vine is a vigorous, deciduous, woody, twining climber. The leaves are opposite, 2.5–5cm/1–2in, oval to lance-shaped, glossy, dark green, turning yellow in autumn. The flowers, up to 2.5cm/1in across with five downy, spreading lobes, are borne in long-stalked corymbs of eight to ten from early to late summer; they have a yellow-green exterior and maroon to chocolate interior. They are followed by pairs of narrowly cylindrical seedpods, up to 12.5cm/5in long.

Distribution: South-east Europe to western Asia.
Height and spread: 10m/33ft.
Habit and form: Woody, twining climber.
Leaf shape: Ovate to lanceolate.
Pollinated: Insect.

Left: Silk vine climbs vigorously by twining around the stems of other plants.

Giant Carrion Flower

Stapelia nobilis

An interesting succulent, found intermittently from South Africa as far north as Tanzania, that has olive-green, erect branches, which give the plant a cactus-like appearance. It bears large, foul-smelling, starfish-shaped flowers that are pale yellow with reddish stripes, covered with white hairs. The flowers are said to look flesh-like and this, when combined with the rotting meat odour, attracts its main visitor, the fly, for pollinating.

Identification: The stems are four-sided, rigid, spineless, 15–20cm/6–8in tall and 3cm/1¼in in diameter. They are pale green and robust, and the angles are winged with small teeth. One or two flowers are borne from the base to midway up the stem, and are 25–35cm/10–14in across, flat to slightly bell-shaped, with a short dark red tube, which is densely wrinkled, and a dark purple-brown corona. The lobes are oval with elongated tapering points, pale ochre-yellow, with many tiny, wavy crimson stripes and fringed with hairs.

Distribution: South Africa to Tanzania.
Height and spread: 15–20cm/6–8in; indefinite spread.
Habit and form: Succulent.
Leaf shape: Absent.
Pollinated: Fly.

Left: The olive-green branches are robust, held erect and lined with small teeth, and give this plant a rather cactus-like appearance.

Pyrenean Violet

Ramonda myconi

Distribution: Pyrenees.
Height and spread:
12.5cm/5in.
Habit and form: Herbaceous
perennial.
Leaf shape: Elliptic to
rhomboidal.
Pollinated: Insect.

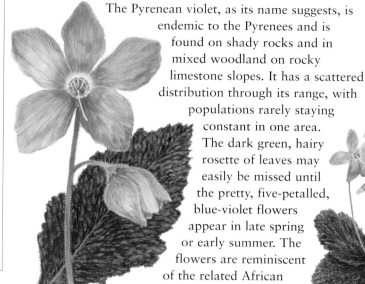

The Pyrenean violet, as its name suggests, is endemic to the Pyrenees and is found on shady rocks and in mixed woodland on rocky limestone slopes. It has a scattered distribution through its range, with populations rarely staying constant in one area. The dark green, hairy rosette of leaves may easily be missed until the pretty, five-petalled, blue-violet flowers appear in late spring or early summer. The flowers are reminiscent of the related African violet, *Saintpaulia* species, to which this plant is distantly related.

Identification: A low-growing, stemless herb, with a basal rosette of wrinkled leaves up to 6cm/2¼in long, elliptic to diamond-shaped with rounded tips and marginal teeth, covered in red-brown hairs. Between one and six flowers are borne on glandular to hairy, red-tinged leafless stalks, up to 12.5cm/5in tall, in early summer. Each five-lobed flower is 4cm/1½in across, violet to pink or white with a yellow, cone-shaped centre.

Left: The leaves are held in a tight basal rosette from where the flowers emerge.

OTHER MILKWEED AND GESNERIAD SPECIES

Hoya sussuela
This vigorous climbing vine from Indonesia has leathery, light green leaves, about 5–10cm/2–4in long, with a clear centre vein. The unusual waxy flowers are cup-shaped, dark maroon with pointed lobes arranged in a star fashion, with up to 10 flowers in an umbel. They have a strong musky odour.

Ceropegia ballyana
This robust, climbing, succulent-rooted vine from Kenya has unusual, green-white flowers with red-brown spots. The base appears triangular in profile and with the twisted tips of the lobes the whole flower looks like a fairy light.

Titanotrichum oldhamii
This pretty plant from Taiwan has a woody rootstock and produces several erect herbaceous stems with yellow, tubular flowers, which are red to maroon on the inside of the tube and borne in terminal racemes during the summer months. Although it bears a passing resemblance to a foxglove it is unrelated.

Chirita lavandulacea
This upright-growing annual species, which is native to tropical Asia, has oval, prominently veined, translucent, hairy leaves that act as a perfect foil for the pretty, five-lobed, pale blue flowers. These are borne on short stalks, singly or in pairs and groups of three to five, from the upper leaf axils.

Cape Primrose

Streptocarpus formosus

More than 100 widespread species of *Streptocarpus* are found mostly in southern Africa. This species grows in subtropical forests where the summers are humid and wet, and the winters are warm and dry. It has a scattered distribution in forests and the sandstone gorges, where it grows in pockets of well-drained soil between the rocks. Surprisingly, each leaf of the clump is an individual plant with its own roots and flowering stems.

Distribution: Central and South Africa, Madagascar.
Height and spread:
25cm/10in.
Habit and form: Rosette-forming, evergreen perennial.
Leaf shape: Oblong.
Pollinated: Insect.

Identification: A rosette-forming perennial with many hairy leaves, up to 45cm/18in long. Each inflorescence, up to 25cm/10in tall, bears one to four pale blue flowers up to 10cm/4in across. The flower tube is narrowly funnel-shaped, blue-mauve outside, the inside minutely spotted purple with a patch of bright yellow and purple streaks on the floor; the lobes are white or blue streaked white. The fruits, 18cm/7in long, unfold like a spiral when dry.

Below: The flowers appear from spring.

Rght: The small perennial is clump-forming.

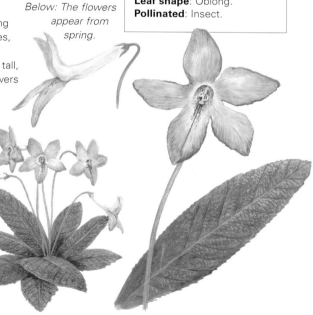

CUCURBIT FAMILY

The Cucurbitaceae are mostly prostrate or climbing herbaceous annuals. The family comprises about 90 genera and 700 species, which are characterized by five-angled stems and coiled tendrils. It is one of the most important families of food plants in the world, including crops such as squashes, gourds, melons and cucumbers. Most of the plants in this family are annual vines with fairly large, showy blossoms.

White Bryony

Common bryony, *Bryonia dioica*

This vine-like plant is common in European woods and hedges. The stems climb by means of long tendrils springing from the side of the leaf stalks, and extend among trees and shrubs, often to the length of several yards during the summer. They die away after the fruit has ripened, although the large tuber survives in the soil and new stems grow the following year.

Right: The berries often persist until after the stems have withered.

Identification: A climbing herbaceous perennial, with tendrils arising from the leaf axils. The stems are angular and brittle, branched mostly at the base, very rough, with short, prickly hairs. The leaves are held on curved stalks, shorter than the blade, and are divided into five, slightly angular lobes, of which the middle lobe is the longest. Small, greenish-white flowers, generally in small bunches of three or four, spring from the axils of the leaves in late spring, with the sexes on separate plants. The plant produces red berries, which are most noticeable after the stems and leaves have withered. The berries are filled with juice with an unpleasant, foetid odour and contain three to six large seeds, which are greyish-yellow mottled with black.

Distribution: Europe.
Height and spread: Up to 5m/16ft.
Habit and form: Herbaceous vine.
Leaf shape: Palmately lobed.
Pollinated: Insect.

Left: Long stems clamber over other plants, attaching to them by means of tendrils.

Ivy Gourd

Scarlet gourd *Coccinia grandis*

Native to Africa, Asia, Fiji, and northern (tropical) Australia, ivy gourd bears white or yellow flowers followed by scarlet fruits with white spots. It is a rapidly growing, climbing or trailing vine. In its native habitat it is a common, but not serious, weed that is kept in check by competing plants and natural enemies. In recent years, it has become an invasive weed in some tropical countries where it has been introduced.

Identification: An aggressive, fast-growing herbaceous perennial vine, with succulent, hairless stems produced annually from a tuberous rootstock, with occasional adventitious roots forming where they run along the ground. Long simple tendrils from the leaf axils wrap around the host plant. The leaves are alternate, smooth, broadly oval, five-lobed, 9cm/3½in long, with a short, pointed tip, heart-shaped base and minutely toothed margins. The white, bell-shaped flowers, 4cm/1½in long, usually solitary, are deeply divided into five oval lobes. The fruit is a smooth, egg-shaped gourd, bright red when ripe, 2.5–6cm/1–2¼in long.

Left: The fast-growing stems quickly smother other plants.

Distribution: Africa, Asia, Fiji and northern Australia.
Height and spread: Up to 30m/100ft.
Habit and form: Herbaceous vine.
Leaf shape: Broadly ovate to cordate.
Pollinated: Insect.

Above right: Bright red fruits give this vine a very distinctive appearance.

Squirting Cucumber

Touch-me-not, exploding cucumber, *Ecballium elaterium*

This member of the Cucurbitaceae is found in most of the Mediterranean region and Macronesia, growing in rich peat with some water and lots of sun. The vine has developed a unique strategy for the spreading of its seeds: while the fruit ripens, pressure develops inside. When the fruit separates from the stalk, for example if it is touched by an animal, the sticky seeds squirt out, hence the name.

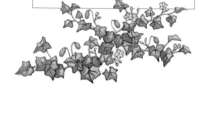

Distribution: Mediterranean region and Atlantic islands.
Height and spread: 30 × 90cm/1 × 3ft.
Habit and form: Trailing, slightly bushy herbaceous perennial.
Leaf shape: Palmately lobed.
Pollinated: Insect.

Below right: The small, hairy seedpods squirt their contents out explosively when ripe.

Identification: A trailing to slightly bushy herbaceous perennial with fleshy, triangular or heart-shaped leaves, palmately lobed, with a bristly upper surface and downy underside. It has yellow funnel- or bell-shaped flowers, about 2.5cm/1in across, sometimes with deeper yellow centres. Both male and female flowers appear on one plant, the male flowers in racemes, the female flowers solitary. The egg-shaped hairy seedpods, which are blue-green and 4–5cm/1½–2in long, enclose many seeds in a watery mucilage that is ejected explosively when the fruit is ripe.

Far left: The trailing stems spread to make a low mat of leafy growth.

OTHER CUCURBIT FAMILY SPECIES

Nara Melon *Acanthosicyos horridus*
A leafless shrub native to the coastal region of the Namib Desert. It forms a densely tangled and spreading mass that can cover up to 1,500m²/1,790yd². Heavily armed with spines 2.5cm/1in long, it grows where underground water is available. Its oil-rich nuts are the staple diet of some of the indigenous Namib people.

Wax Gourd *Benincasa hispida*
The wax gourd or winter melon is a trailing, fleshy vine, grown in many warm countries for its edible fruits. Its solitary yellow flowers are followed by melon- or cucumber-shaped fruit. It probably originated in China and now exists as a garden escapee across much of Asia and beyond.

Watermelon *Citrullus lanatus*
The watermelon grows widely in Africa and Asia, and in the Kalahari Desert the wild melons have been an important source of water and food to indigenous inhabitants, as well as explorers. The history of their domestication is obscure but a wide variety of watermelons have been cultivated in Africa since antiquity.

Cretan Bryony
Bryonia cretica
Similar to white bryony, of which it is sometimes considered to be a subspecies, Cretan bryony has a more southerly distribution. The Cretan bryony has red berries.

Tatior-pot

Ma kling, *Hodgsonia heteroclita*

This large woody climbing plant, from the tropical forests of South-east Asia, is cultivated as a food plant for its large fleshy fruits, which are similar to pumpkin, and its extremely oily seeds. It is rare in the wild, and many populations are considered endangered. Flowering starts at night and continues into the following day.

Identification: Up to 30m/100ft in height or spread, this climber has leaves that are deeply three or five-lobed, almost smooth with a few small glands. Climbing tendrils have two or three branches. The male and female inflorescences are separate: males are 15–35cm/6–14in long, on a 8–15cm/3–6in stalk bearing 10–20 pale yellow, velvety, five-lobed flowers, each 3–5cm/1¼–2in long. The female flowers resemble the males but are solitary. The fruits are 15–20cm/6–8in in diameter, greenish-brown turning red-brown, smooth or shallowly grooved.

Above right: The oil-rich seeds can be eaten.

Distribution: Widely scattered in Sikkim, Bhutan, east India, south China, Burma, Indochina and Thailand.
Height and spread: Up to 30m/100ft.
Habit and form: Woody climbing plant.
Leaf shape: Palmately lobed.
Pollinated: Insect.

Below: Hodgsonia heteroclita is a vine.

CARNIVOROUS PLANTS

Strictly, carnivorous plants are those that attract, capture, kill and digest animals and absorb the nutrients from them. They are by no means common, but several plant families have become specialists in this way of life. There are various ways in which plants have adapted to do this. Most carnivorous plants are small or medium-sized herbaceous perennials; a few are woody climbers.

Round-leaved Sundew

Drosera rotundifolia

This is an unmistakable plant with a widespread distribution. It is a small, short-lived, insectivorous herbaceous perennial, most often found in acidic bogs, but also in swamps, rotting logs, mossy crevices in rocks, or damp sand along stream, lake, or pond margins. It is generally associated with sphagnum mosses, growing on floating sphagnum mats or hummocks. The plant compensates for the low level of nutrients available in its habitat by catching and digesting insects. The prey is caught on the sticky glandular leaf hairs, and the leaf then folds around it. The hairs secrete enzymes that digest the insect and enable the plant to absorb nutrients through its leaves.

Identification: The leaves form a basal rosette, with their round, depressed blades lying flat on the ground; the upper surface of each blade, 6–10mm/¼–½in long, is covered with reddish, glandular hairs, each tipped with a sticky, glutinous secretion resembling a dewdrop, which traps insects. The leaf stalk is 2–5cm/¾–2in long and covered with sticky hairs. One-sided racemes, one to seven per rosette, consist of 2–15 small white flowers on 5–15cm/2–6in stalks, which straighten out as the flowers expand in summer.

Distribution: Europe, Asia, South Africa, North and South America.
Height and spread: 5–15cm/2–6in.
Habit and form: Herbaceous perennial.
Leaf shape: Orbicular.
Pollinated: Insect.

Greater Bladderwort

Utricularia vulgaris

Bladderworts are carnivorous aquatic plants with delicate, finely divided underwater leaves and emergent, snapdragon-like yellow flowers. Their most distinctive underwater features are small, bladder-like traps – oval balloons with a double-sealed airtight door on one end. When the door is closed, the bladder expels water through its walls, creating a partial vacuum inside, which sucks in small invertebrates or even tiny fish that trigger the trap doors. Enzymes are secreted to digest the prey and provide the plant with nutrients. Bladderworts are most commonly found floating freely in shallow water, or loosely attached to sediment, and are widely distributed throughout Europe, North Africa and the USA.

Left and far right: Flowering stems rise above the water, while the rest of the foliage remains under the surface.

Above right: The tiny bladders capture small aquatic invertebrates.

Identification: This water-living, herbaceous plant has no true leaves or roots. Instead, it has a green, finely divided, underwater leaf-like stem with small, seed-like bladders. The branched stem is up to 2m/6½ft long and can be floating, submersed, or partly creeping on sediment, sometimes anchored at the base by root-like structures. It overwinters above the sediment layer. Yellow, snapdragon-like flowers, up to 2.5cm/1in wide, have a prominent spur projecting below the lower lip and faint purple-brown stripes; they are held above the water on stout stalks in late summer. The globular brown seed capsules contain many seeds. The winter bud is ovoid to ellipsoid, to 2cm/¾in long.

Distribution: Europe, North Africa and North America.
Height and spread: 15–45cm x 2m/6–18in x 6½ft.
Habit and form: Water plant.
Leaf shape: No true leaves.
Pollinated: Insect.

OTHER CARNIVOROUS PLANT SPECIES

Great Sundew Drosera anglica
The great sundew is similar to the round-leaved sundew but with taller and narrower leaves, about twice as long as they are wide. It is generally found in the same habitat and range as the round-leaved sundew but is much less common.

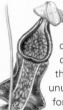

Nepenthes rafflesiana
This pitcher plant has cream-coloured traps nearly covered in dark red botches. It is distributed throughout Borneo and is an unusually variable plant, with various forms looking like completely different species. The pitchers are often visited by ants but the plant seems not to be specialized in its prey.

Drosera cistiflora
This very striking South African sundew has long, fine leaves and an erect habit, growing to 25cm/10in or more before producing several large, typically pink, flowers. There is also a giant form up to 50cm/20in tall and forms with different flower colours are known.

Roridula gorgonias
This perennial from South Africa, which grows to around 50cm/20in, is covered with sticky glands, which capture insects much as sundews do. The plants do not assimilate the nutrients from the dead insects they catch; instead, assassin bugs in the genus Pameridea eat the insects and their excrement is absorbed by the leaves.

Greater Butterwort

Pinguicula grandiflora

Greater butterwort grows throughout much of the Northern Hemisphere. It is distinct in having one of the most striking flowers of the butterwort family (Lentibulariaceae) and superficially resembles a small African violet, *Saintpaulia* species, although they are unrelated. Greater butterwort is a small plant that grows in a rosette fashion, and has tiny transparent hairs that secrete sticky glue. There are also glands on the leaves, which are dry until an insect is captured. They then secrete acids and enzymes, which start to dissolve the insect before the same glands reabsorb the nutrient-rich fluid.

Distribution: Arctic Circle, Europe, Siberia and North America.
Height and spread: 15cm/6in.
Habit and form: Herbaceous perennial.
Leaf shape: Obovate-oblong.
Pollinated: Insect.

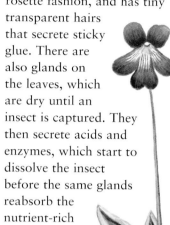

Identification: The plant forms a rosette of oval to oblong, sticky, pale green leaves 3–5cm/1¼–2in long, with resting buds in the winter. In summer, solitary, trumpet-shaped, spurred, two-lipped, dark blue flowers, 2.5cm/1in across, with three widely spreading lobes and white throats, are borne on slender stems.

Pitcher Plant

Nepenthes ampullaria

Distribution: Lowlands of South-east Asia.
Height and spread: Up to 20m/65ft.
Habit and form: Woody liana.
Leaf shape: Lanceolate, sometimes ending in a pitcher.
Pollinated: Insect.

This carnivorous plant, native to swamps in the humid tropical lowlands of South-east Asia, is a woody vine that forms rosettes of trapping leaves. In its native habitat, the rosettes may arise anywhere along the vine, although in mature plants large clumps of pitchers form at the base of the climbing stem. These fill with rainwater and insects that fall into them, and drown; their decaying bodies yield nutrients absorbed by the plant.

Identification: A woody liana, with rounded, squat, deep red or green, sometimes mottled pitchers, up to 10cm/4in high, with round, horizontal mouths and narrow, reflexed lids that allow the broad pitchers to fill with rainwater. Wings on the front of the pitcher are broad, spreading and toothed. The basal traps are numerous and squat, with upper ones few and more cylindrical in shape, often with a dusty appearance due to a thick coating of fine hairs. Tiny, petal-less flowers with green-and-brown sepals are borne in spidery racemes. The shape and colour of the pitchers varies considerably according to location.

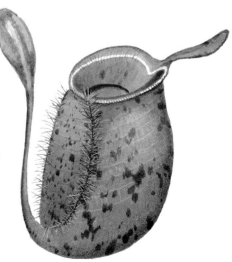

Left: Modified leaves form pitchers, which capture and digest unsuspecting insects.

PARASITIC PLANTS

When one organism "steals" all of its food from another's body, it is called a parasite. The organism that is being robbed of its food supply is known as the host. The parasitic mode of existence can be found from bacteria and fungi to insects, mites and worms. Parasitism has also evolved in many families of flowering plants, and while many of them are quite unrelated, their lifestyle brings them together here.

Rafflesia

Rafflesia manillana

Dramatic and solitary rafflesia flowers are the largest single flowers in the world, with leathery petals that in some species can reach more than 90cm/3ft across. A parasite that depends completely upon its host, the majority of the plant's tissues exist as thread-like strands entirely within vines of *Tetrastigma* species. The rafflesia plant is itself not visible until the flowers first bud through the woody vine, taking up to ten months to develop. The enormous flowers reportedly have a strong smell of rotting flesh and are believed to be pollinated by flies, although it is rarely encountered and its exact life cycle is obscure.

Identification: Only the flower ever emerges for the purposes of identification. It consists of five orange leathery petals, mottled with cream warts. There is a deep well in the centre of the flower containing a central raised disc, which supports many vertical spines. The sexual organs are located beneath the rim of the disc, and male and female flowers are separate. *R. manillana* has a flower 15–20cm/6–8in in diameter; it is the smallest of all rafflesia species.

Distribution: South-east Asia.
Height and spread: 15–20cm/6–8in (flower only).
Habit and form: Internal parasite.
Leaf shape: Absent.
Pollinated: Fly.

Cytinus hypocistis

This parasitic plant, found in Mediterranean forest and coastal scrub, lives on a shrub, the sage-leaved rock rose, *Cistus salviifolius.* Like many other parasites, it takes all its nourishment from the roots of its host and so has no need of leaves or other conventional green plant parts. It reveals itself only at flowering time, when its tight clusters of small very showy flowers erupt from the ground beneath the host plant.

Identification: Orange-and-yellow unisexual flowers are borne singly or in clusters of five to ten at the apex of the flower spike in an umbellate pattern, appearing in spring to early summer. They are subtended by (usually) two bracts and have four bright yellow petaloid sepals, up to 12mm/½in long. The short flower stem is covered with yellow, orange or bright red, densely overlapping scales, resulting from vestigial leaves. Due to their low-growing nature, the flowers can often be hidden by leaf litter.

Distribution: Mediterranean, North Africa, Turkey.
Height and spread: 4–8cm/1½–3¼in (flower only).
Habit and form: Internal parasite.
Leaf shape: Vestigial scales.
Pollinated: Insect.

Left: The tight clusters of showy flowers are the only part of this plant that may be seen above ground.

European Mistletoe

Viscum album

Distribution: Europe.
Height and spread: Up to 90cm/3ft.
Habit and form: Aerial hemi-parasite.
Leaf shape: Elliptic.
Pollinated: Possibly wind or insect.

Far right: European mistletoe lives on many deciduous tree species, particularly fruit trees such as apple, and lime, poplar and oak.

Centuries of superstition and belief are attached to mistletoe, and the tradition of "kissing under the mistletoe" has persisted for many years. It is a partial or hemi-parasite, relying on a host tree to provide it with a growing platform and some nutrients, though it does have chlorophyll in its leaves and can manufacture some food for itself through photosynthesis. The generic name *Viscum* refers to the stickiness of the seeds, a property essential to the plant's propagation method, as its seed must stick to the trunk of its host long enough to germinate and insert a root into the bark.

Identification: The leaves, borne on repeatedly forked branches, are evergreen and elliptical in shape. Male and female flowers are borne on separate plants, with the flowers of both sexes produced in the forks of the branches. Males flower between late winter and mid-spring, producing small clusters of blooms with four petals; the female plants produce sticky white berries in autumn.

OTHER PARASITIC PLANT SPECIES
Red-berried Mistletoe *Viscum cruciatum*
A native of the Mediterranean, the red-berried mistletoe, although closely allied to *V. album*, prefers a warmer and drier climate. It is very similar in shape and form to *V. album* and grows on a range of deciduous trees, especially olives.

Toothwort *Lathraea squamaria*
Also known as corpse flower, this is a perennial parasitic plant, up to 20cm/8in tall, with a pinkish-cream stem and scale-like, fleshy leaves, said to resemble pointed teeth. Flower spikes with cylindrical, half-nodding, pink flowers on one side appear in copses and shady places in spring.

Common Dodder *Cuscuta epithymum*
This small parasitic plant, containing no chlorophyll, appears as a mass of tiny, red strings all over gorse, *Ulex* species, thyme, *Thymus* species, or other low-growing plants that act as its host. Small spherical bunches of little pale pink flowers appear in summer. Seeds sprout in the soil, but wither once it attaches to its host.

Loxanthera speciosa
This unusual, large, woody shrub, with branches to over 3m/10ft, is an aerial hemi-parasite, with large, red-and-white tubular flowers. It grows in forest in Malaysia, Sumatra, Java and Borneo, on host trees such as the tiup tiup, *Adinandra dumosa*, and several *Ficus* species, between sea level and 850m/2,800ft.

Purple Toothwort

Lathraea clandestina

This spreading perennial, found in the damp woods and streamside meadows of south-western Europe, grows as a parasite on the roots of willow, alder and poplar trees. The plant does not produce true leaves but vestigial leaves still occur in the form of fleshy scales on the rhizomes. The purple flowers, which appear in spring, are the only parts visible above ground, but colonies of the plant may have an indefinite spread. It is found widely in temperate regions, having been imported with garden trees.

Identification: A parasitic, rhizomatous perennial, with opposite, kidney-shaped, stem-clasping, scale-like white leaves, 5mm/⅕in long. Dense racemes of between four and eight hooded, tubular, two-lipped mauve flowers, to 3cm/1¼in long, are borne just above the ground in early and mid-spring.

Distribution: South-west Europe.
Height and spread: 2cm/¾in; indefinite spread.
Habit and form: Root parasite.
Leaf shape: Reniform scale.
Pollinated: Bumblebee.

Right: The mauve flowers are showy with an upper lip that has a hooded shape.

Below: The flowers that appear in spring are the only visible parts, but colonies may be quite extensive.

DUCKWEED AND ARUM FAMILIES

The duckweed family (Lemnaceae) contains mostly perennial, aquatic, floating or submersed herbs that are reduced to small green bodies. The Araceae are rhizomatous or tuberous herbaceous perennials. They are characterized by an inflorescence that is a fleshy spadix partially enveloped by a bract or spathe that is sometimes brightly coloured.

Lesser Duckweed

Lemna minor

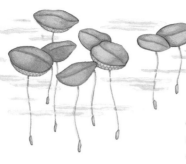

This tiny, floating, aquatic perennial, which often forms a seemingly solid cover on the water surface, is made up of many tiny individual plants. It is widespread throughout the temperate regions of the Northern Hemisphere, including North America and Eurasia, being absent only from polar areas and the tropics. It occurs chiefly in freshwater ponds, marshes, lakes and quiet streams. It is able to spread most rapidly across quiet bodies of water rich in nutrients, such as nitrogen and phosphate. Flowering duckweeds are uncommon.

Below: Lesser duckweed seems to form a blanket over water.

Identification: The tiny individual plants may be up to 15mm/⅝in across, but are usually 2–4mm/1/16–⅛in. Their leaves and stems are merged in a simple, three-lobed plant body, typically called a frond or "thallus", though neither term is botanically precise. The frond consists of one to several layers of conspicuous air spaces and one to several veins. It is flattened, round to elliptic-oval in outline, generally symmetrical, with a smooth upper surface. A single root hangs down in the water.

Distribution: Temperate areas worldwide.
Height and spread: Unlimited spread over suitable water habitat.
Habit and form: Floating aquatic perennial.
Leaf shape: Rounded.
Pollinated: None.

Right: The flowers are microscopic.

Left: The small fronds form a dense floating mass.

Dragon Arum

Voodoo lily, *Dracunculus vulgaris*

This rather bizarre plant, unique to the Mediterranean region, is reminiscent of an arum lily. It can be found growing in well-drained soils and full sun. It produces a spathe that, as it unfurls, reveals a slender, black central appendage, the spadix, which can reach 25–135cm/ 10–53in in length. The actual flowers, both male and female, are hidden deep inside the spathe, which features a bulbous chamber. It relies on flies and other insects for pollination and therefore emits a putrid smell, like dung and carrion, to attract them.

Identification: Unmistakable by sight or smell, this tuberous perennial with foot-shaped or spear-shaped, dark green basal leaves, 30cm/12in or more long, has a stem marked purple-brown. In spring or summer, foul-smelling, maroon-purple spathes, 60–100cm/24–39in long, with erect, almost black spadices, are borne above the leaves, attracting large numbers of beetles and flies, which become trapped in the spathe chamber.

Left: The flowering stem is a dramatic sight once the bloom opens.

Distribution: Southern Europe to Turkey.
Height and spread: Up to 1.8m/6ft.
Habit and form: Herbaceous perennial.
Leaf shape: Pedate or hastate.
Pollinated: Insect.

Left: Clusters of fruit surround the remains of the flower spike.

White Arum Lily

Calla lily, *Zantedeschia aethiopica*

This plant is neither an arum (genus *Arum*) nor a lily (genus *Lilium*). It was introduced to Europe in the 17th century, and has naturalized in almost all parts of the world. The striking flower is made up of many tiny flowers arranged in a complex spiral pattern on the central spadix, the top 7.5cm/3in of which are male flowers with the lower 2cm/¾in being female. The whiteness of the spathe is caused by an optical effect produced by numerous airspaces beneath the epidermis. Its flowering season depends upon its location; plants in the Western Cape are dormant in summer, while in the eastern summer rainfall areas the species is dormant in winter, although it remains evergreen if growing in marshy conditions that are wet all year round.

Distribution: South Africa.
Height and spread: 90cm/3ft.
Habit and form: Herbaceous perennial.
Leaf shape: Sagittate.
Pollinated: Insect.

Left: The foliage forms a clump in wet soil.

Identification: A clump-forming, rhizomatous, usually evergreen perennial, it has semi-erect, arrow-shaped, glossy bright green leaves up to 40cm/16in long. Flowers are borne in succession, and are large, pure white spathes, to 25cm/10in long, with creamy-yellow spadices. The spathe turns green after flowering and covers the ripening, succulent yellow berries.

Left: The white flowers are extremely striking.

OTHER DUCKWEED AND ARUM SPECIES

Wolffia microscopica
Wolffias are the smallest flowering plants on earth. They are native across subtropical and tropical India. This tiny aquatic plant has one of the most rapid rates of vegetative reproduction, producing a smaller daughter plant every 30–36 hours.

Pink Calla *Zantedeschia rehmannii*
The pink calla, or pink arum, produces white, pink or violet-red spathes, with yellow spadices, growing up among the lance-shaped, dark green leaves to 40cm/16in, and leaves that are blotched with white or semitransparent spots. In its native South Africa it is a naturally quite variable species.

Lords and Ladies *Arum maculatum*
This arum, also known as cuckoo pint, first becomes apparent in midwinter, when its narrow, green spathes emerge from the ground. The flowers open in mid- to late spring, then the hood decays leaving a stem on which bright red berries develop and ripen in the autumn.

Titan Arum *Amorphophallus titanium*
Found only in the equatorial tropical rainforests of Sumatra, Indonesia, the titan arum is estimated to be the largest inflorescence in nature. The spadix can reach more than 1.8m/6ft tall, with the spathe reaching about 90cm/3ft across. The single leaf can reach 6m/20ft tall and 4.5m/15ft across.

Cobra Lily

Arisaema candidissimum

This tuberous perennial from China is found on stony slopes and in open pine forests, in full sun, on dry, rocky, south-facing slopes. Cobra lilies emerge in late spring with stalks of pink pitcher flowers, which are striped with translucent, white, vertical veins. The central flower spike is male or female, with the tip slightly bent. Alongside the flower emerges a three-lobed leaf, which can reach up to 60cm/2ft wide.

Identification: In summer the plant bears a conspicuous, sweetly scented, pink-striped white spathe, striped green on the outside, 7.5–15cm/3–6in long with a hooked, downward-curling tip. The inflorescence is up to 12.5cm/5in tall, depending upon habitat. A solitary, three-palmate, mid- to deep green leaf, very thick and leathery, with broadly oval leaflets, each 10–25cm/4–10in long and almost as broad, appears on a leaf stalk up to 35cm/14in tall, only after the spathe emerges.

Distribution: Chinese Himalayas.
Height and spread: 40cm/16in.
Habit and form: Herbaceous perennial.
Leaf shape: Palmate.
Pollinated: Insect.

Right: The greenish exterior of the flower belies the candy-striped interior.

Below: The single, large tri-lobed leaf appears only after the flower bud has emerged.

BANANA, STRELITZIA AND GINGER FAMILIES

The Musaceae, or banana family, are large, often tree-like herbaceous perennials. Closely allied to this family is Strelitziaceae, native to tropical south-eastern Africa and Madagascar. Zingiberaceae, or ginger, are herbaceous perennials, mostly with creeping horizontal or tuberous rhizomes, with a wide distribution.

Abyssinian Banana

Wild banana, red banana, *Ensete ventricosum*

Often wrongly described as trees, bananas are, in fact, giant herbaceous plants, the "trunk" (technically a pseudostem) being made up of a series of tightly wrapped leaf sheaths. Each pseudostem grows from a bud on the true stem, which is an underground rhizome. Leaves emerge through the centre of the pseudostem and expand at the top to form large, glossy, oval blades, up to 4 x 1m/ 13 x 3ft in size. *E. ventricosum*, a relative of the edible bananas, *Musa* species, is a highly variable species with a large African range. The fruit is not eaten except in times of scarcity, but the young flowers are palatable when cooked.

Identification: The plant, though herbaceous, is tall and tree-like, with a pseudostem up to 5m/16ft, often variably stained purple, with whitish latex that reddens on exposure to air. The oblong to lance-shaped leaves are borne on short stalks in a banana-like crown, erect or spreading, bright yellow-green or variably stained with red-brown, more or less glaucous beneath. The midribs are green, red or purple-brown. A drooping inflorescence bears a massive male bud. Mature fruits are banana-like but dry, bright yellow or yellow-orange with orange pulp. It seldom forms suckers from the base (as in other species) and is monocarpic.

Distribution: Africa.
Height and spread: 4–12m/13–40ft.
Habit and form: Tall herbaceous but tree-like plant.
Leaf shape: Oblong-lanceolate.
Pollinated: Insect.

Left: Flowerheads appear when plants are about eight years old.

Bird of Paradise

Crane flower, *Strelitzia reginae*

Possibly one of the best-known plants in the world, the strelitzia's fascinating blooms are sold as cut flowers by the million and this popularity has led them to be grown in gardens worldwide. *S. reginae* is, however, indigenous to South Africa, where it grows wild in the Eastern Cape, between other shrubs along the riverbanks and in clearings in the coastal bush. Mature plants can form large clumps in favourable conditions and are very floriferous, with flowers in autumn, winter and spring. When birds visit the flowers to help themselves to nectar, the petals open and cover their feet in pollen.

Identification: A large, clump-forming, nearly stemless evergreen perennial, with erect, oblong to lance-shaped stiff grey-green leaves with pointed or rounded tips, sometimes with a shallow notch at the end, to around 90cm/3ft long. The flowers, borne on long, sheathed stalks, emerge from a glaucous, horizontal spathe about 12.5cm/5in long, green flushed purple and orange; the flowers are about 10cm/4in long, with orange sepals and blue, narrowly arrow-shaped petals, with rounded basal lobes.

Distribution: South Africa.
Height and spread: Up to 2m/6½ft.
Habit and form: Stemless evergreen perennial.
Leaf shape: Oblong-lanceoleate.
Pollinated: Bird.

Left: Large clumps of leafy growth appear from the underground stems.

Dwarf Savanna Ginger Lily

Costus spectabilis

Distribution: Tropical Africa.
Height and spread:
10cm/4in.
Habit and form:
Rhizomatous perennial.
Leaf shape: Ovate-lanceolate.
Pollinated: Insect.

Costus is a large genus with more than 100 species distributed in the tropical rainforests, mainly in Africa and South America. The dwarf savanna ginger lily, found in humid or semi-humid savannas all over tropical Africa, from Senegal to the eastern coastal zones, has one of the largest blooms of all, the showy yellow flowers being highly visible during the flowering period. The plant can easily be missed when not in flower, however, as it is a low, ground-hugging species. The plants remain naturally dormant and inconspicuous during the dry season, and flowering does not occur until after the traditional burning of grassland at the beginning of the rainy season.

Identification: A rhizomatous perennial, largely stemless above the ground. The long snake-like rhizomes grow during the dry season and give rise to four-leaved spiral rosettes, that are flat on the ground. The leaves are pale green with red edges, obovate-cuneate, smooth above, downy below and cupped. Three to four bright yellow or bright orange flowers, located terminally, appear at the centre of the rosette. The fruit is a membranous capsule crowned by a persistent calyx.

OTHER BANANA, STRELITZIA AND GINGER SPECIES

Japanese Banana *Musa basjoo*
Despite its name, the Japanese banana is a medium-size species from China, growing to about 2.5m/8ft tall before flowering, though it may become considerably taller with age. The leaves are bright, light green, sometimes with a reddish flush to the underside.

Aframomum sceptrum
Generally restricted to deep forest habitats in West Africa, the Congo and Angola, the 30cm/12in inflorescences of this species arise at the base of, or independently some distance away from, the tall and leafy shoots, clothed in 25cm/10in long sheathing leaves.

Ginger *Zingiber officinale*
Ginger is a herb indigenous to South-east Asia, although it is widely cultivated in the USA, India, China, West Indies and tropical regions. The plant is a creeping perennial on a thick tuberous rhizome, with narrow, deciduous lance-shaped leaves and a long, curved spike of white or yellow flowers.

Cardamom *Elettaria cardamomum*
Common in southern India and Sri Lanka, cardamom is a perennial plant. The simple, erect stems grow to 3m/10ft from a thumb-thick, creeping rootstock. The small, yellowish flowers, which grow on prostrate stems, are followed by the capsules, which are used as a culinary spice.

Green Ripple Peacock Ginger

Kaempferia elegans

This plant is native to areas of Thailand, East Bengal, Burma and those parts of the Malay Peninsula with pronounced dry seasons, and is naturally deciduous. All *Kaempferia* species tend to be short, unlike many other plants in the Zingiberaceae. They are most notable for their foliage, which is often patterned and multicoloured, resulting in the common name of peacock ginger. The flowers, although usually inconspicuous, are a very pretty lilac. All the aerial parts die down in the dry season; the plant vegetates solely during the wet season.

Distribution: Southern Asia.
Height and spread: 15–20 x 30cm/6–8 x 12in.
Habit and form: Deciduous, rhizomatous herb.
Leaf shape: Oblong or elliptic.
Pollinated: Insect.

Identification: A low-growing, deciduous, rhizomatous herb. The smooth leaves are oblong or elliptic, broad and wavy, up to 15cm/6in long, with a pointed tip and rounded base, on short stalks. Lilac flowers with 5cm/2in green bracts appear almost daily amid the leaves during the summer months.

IRIS FAMILY

The Iridaceae are herbaceous perennials growing from rhizomes, bulbs or corms and occurring in tropical and temperate regions, particularly around the Mediterranean, in South Africa and Central America. The flowers are single and almost stemless (as in Crocus*), or occur as spikes at the top of branched or unbranched stems, each with six petals in two rings of three. Many are ornamental.*

Yellow Flag

Iris pseudacorus

A robust plant with beautiful, bright yellow flowers that occurs throughout much of Europe, North Africa, western Asia and the Caucasus. It has become widely naturalized outside its original range, as a garden escapee. It is common in wet habitats, including meadows, woods, fens, wet dune-slacks, and the edges of watercourses, lakes and ponds. In some areas it may also be found alongside coastal streams, on raised beaches, in saltmarsh and shingle.

Identification: An extremely vigorous, rhizomatous, beardless water iris. The 90cm/3ft leaves are ribbed, with an especially prominent midrib, grey-green, broad, flat, sword-shaped and stalkless, with several bound together into a sheath at the base. In mid- and late summer, each branched, somewhat flattened stem bears four to seven showy flowers, 7.5–10cm/3–4in across, from very large pointed buds. The petals are yellow with brown or violet markings and a darker yellow zone on each fall. The roots are thick and fleshy, brownish on the outside, reddish and spongy within, pushing through moist ground parallel to the surface, with many rootlets passing downward.

Distribution: Europe, North Africa, western Asia and the Caucasus.
Height and spread: 90cm/3ft.
Habit and form: Rhizomatous perennial.
Leaf shape: Linear-lanceolate.
Pollinated: Bee.

Left: The tall flower spikes are often seen beside water among other vegetation.

Right: The seedpod.

Crocus vernus *ssp.* albiflorus

This form of *Crocus vernus* is the smaller, high mountain plant, often seen in spring to midsummer in the Alps and the Pyrenees, although the species may be found more widely in Central and Southern Europe. It is restricted to mountain turf in areas where there is a decidedly cold winter and a short alpine summer, with snow cover persisting until well into spring, and it can often be seen flowering as the snow melts in spring or summer. The flower is commonly white but can also be purple or striped. It rarely hybridizes with the other subspecies *C. vernus* ssp. *vernus*, even when populations overlap, as both occupy different habitats.

Identification: An herbaceous corm that in time forms extensive colonies. Dull, green, semi-erect to linear-lance-shaped leaves, with pale silvery-green central stripes, appearing in spring at the same time as the flowers, can be glabrous or pubescent; elongating markedly as the flowers fade. The single white, goblet-shaped flowers, varying from pure white to being marked with purple, have a yellow style and anthers.

Distribution: Mediterranean, Balkans and south-west Asia.
Height and spread: 7–15cm/3–6in.
Habit and form: Herbaceous corm.
Leaf shape: Linear-lanceolate.
Pollinated: Insect.

Left and above left: The white flowers of this subspecies are borne singly at the same time as the leaves.

Right: Flowers may be white or can be marked with purple.

Waterfall Gladiolus

New Year Lily, *Gladiolus cardinalis*

The genus *Gladiolus* comprises about 180 species of cormous perennials that originate mainly in South Africa but also in western and central Europe, central Asia, north-west and east Africa. This species from South Africa, known as the waterfall gladiolus, is often found growing under waterfalls and, as its other common name suggests, is in bloom there in December to January, although it is now thought to be virtually extinct in the wild. The plant that is grown as a cultivated form is not the true species, but the result of cross-breeding.

Identification: A cormous perennial with flattened corms and narrow to broadly sword-shaped leaves produced in fan-like tufts. In summer, arching, one-sided spikes bear up to 12 widely funnel-shaped, bright red flowers, 5cm/2in across, with white patches in the lip tepals. Each flower has six tepals: usually one central upper tepal, three smaller lower or lip tepals and two side or wing tepals. Flowers open from the base of the spike, with the older flowers dying as new ones develop and open.

Distribution: South Africa.
Height and spread: 40–90cm/16–36in.
Habit and form: Cormous perennial.
Leaf shape: Linear-lanceolate.
Pollinated: Insect.

Right: The plant has strap-like leaves.

Far right: The tall flower stems are clothed in large flowers that are red.

OTHER IRIS FAMILY SPECIES

Iris lortetii
This extremely showy iris is found in Israel, Syria and northern Iraq, in areas where the rainy season is short and drought may occur for extended periods. It is 30–50cm/12–20in tall, with white flowers veined and dotted pink or maroon, deep maroon signals and mauve falls, speckled brownish-red.

Green Ixia *Ixia viridiflora*
From South Africa, the green ixia is one of the taller ixias, with upright, narrow, grass-like leaves, 40–55cm/16–22in long, surrounding a lax, many-flowered spike up to 90cm/3ft tall. Each flower is a brilliant turquoise-green with a conspicuous purple-black, circular stain or "eye" in the middle.

Table Mountain Watsonia *Watsonia tabularis*
The Table Mountain watsonia, native to the Western Cape, bears striking stalks, 1.2–1.5m/4–5ft tall, of arching, goblet-shaped blooms, in a range of colours from deep rose to salmon-orange, that appear between late spring and midsummer and are especially abundant the season after a fire.

Iris kumaonensis
Native to the western Himalayas, at altitudes between 2,400–5,500m/8,000–18,000ft, this iris has leaves 45cm/18in long and 12mm/½in broad, although at flowering time in the spring they are only 10–15cm/4–6in long around the large, pink-purple-veined flowers.

River Lily

Hesperantha coccinea

Once known as *Schizostylis coccinea*, this handsome plant from Transkei, South Africa, reaches 60–90cm/2–3ft tall, with flowers borne in profusion in autumn. The name *Hesperantha* means "evening flower", and the genus comprises 65 species, which are distributed through both the summer and winter rainfall areas of South Africa. The river lily is a species from the summer rainfall area and is widely distributed through the eastern provinces of the country, found chiefly along river edges and in water meadows, growing in full sun. The flowers are pollinated by butterflies and flies.

Identification: This vigorous, evergreen, clump-forming, rhizomatous perennial has erect, keeled, narrow sword-shaped leaves, up to 40cm/16in long, with distinct midribs. Spikes of 4–14 open, cup-shaped, scarlet flowers, 2cm/¾in across, on a one-sided, 60cm/24in spike, opening from the base upward, are produced in late summer and autumn. There are also pink and white forms.

Distribution: Transkei, South Africa.
Height and spread: 60–90 x 60cm/2–3 x 2ft.
Habit and form: Rhizomatous perennial.
Leaf shape: Linear-lanceolate.
Pollinated: *Aerpetes* butterfly and proboscid flies.

Below: The star-like, scarlet flowers are borne on tall spikes in late summer.

AMARYLLIS FAMILY

The Amaryllidaceae, or amaryllis family, are herbaceous perennials from bulbs with contractile roots, comprising 50 genera and 870 species, which are found mainly in South Africa. Some also grow in South America and in the Mediterranean. The flower usually consists of six distinct or fused petaloid tepals, often with only a single flower on each stalk. Many species in this family have spectacular flowers.

Daffodil

Lenten lily, *Narcissus pseudonarcissus*

The wild daffodil is native to moist shady sites in western Europe at altitudes below 200m/650ft in light woodland. Its presence is generally considered to be a good indicator that the woodland is ancient. Cultivated daffodils are widespread in gardens and elsewhere but the distribution of wild populations is patchy, although where they do grow they tend to be abundant and make a fine display in spring.

Right: Plants produce seed but spread mainly through offsets.

Left: Older bulbs form clumps as they become established.

Identification: Thick, linear, mid-green, grass-like leaves, up to 20cm/8in high, appear at the same time as the flowers. The pale yellow flowers are usually solitary, held horizontally, and consist of six similar, yellow or white spreading perianth segments and a tubular golden-yellow corolla. Cultivated varieties of this species are widely planted and are naturalized in the wild, so distinguishing true wild populations can be difficult. The native plants always have a darker yellow flower tube and slightly twisted tepals, and the flowers are generally smaller and more nodding than in cultivated varieties.

Distribution: Western Europe.
Height and spread: 30cm/1ft.
Habit and form: Deciduous bulbous perennial.
Leaf shape: Linear.
Pollinated: Insect.

Snowdrop

Galanthus nivalis

This pretty little bulbous plant is native across much of Europe, although it is most plentiful in the eastern Mediterranean region. It is widely distributed from Spain to Russia, with several varieties and subspecies much planted in gardens outside its range and consequently found as garden escapees. Usually growing in large drifts on the banks of rivers and streams, in woodland and in damp grassland, it flowers during winter and early spring. The aptly named small flowers often push up through the snow and are white with pale green markings on their petals.

Right: The snowdrop is one of the earliest blooming bulbs, often appearing in midwinter in deciduous woodland.

Identification: Narrow, linear to strap-shaped, blue-green leaves appear at the same time as the flowers. The faintly honey-scented flowers are solitary, pendulous, to 2cm/¾in long, and appear in winter to early spring depending upon their location. The outer perianth segments are much larger than the inner ones, which do not spread on opening but form a cup containing the stamens; the inner perianth segments have a green patch towards their tip.

Distribution: Europe.
Height and spread: Up to 12.5cm/5in.
Habit and form: Deciduous bulbous perennial.
Leaf shape: Narrow linear.
Pollinated: Insect.

Left: The seedhead is a conspicuous green capsule.

Right: Snowdrops form dense clumps of foliage and flower in the late winter.

Cape Flower

Guernsey lily, Japanese spider lily, *Nerine bowdenii*

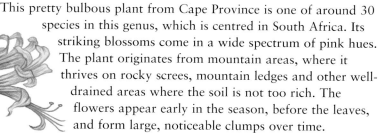

This pretty bulbous plant from Cape Province is one of around 30 species in this genus, which is centred in South Africa. Its striking blossoms come in a wide spectrum of pink hues. The plant originates from mountain areas, where it thrives on rocky screes, mountain ledges and other well-drained areas where the soil is not too rich. The flowers appear early in the season, before the leaves, and form large, noticeable clumps over time.

Distribution: Western Cape, South Africa.
Height and spread: 45cm/18in.
Habit and form: Deciduous bulbous perennial.
Leaf shape: Linear.
Pollinated: Insect.

Identification: Narrow, strap-like, glossy, mid- to dark green leaves, to 30cm/12in, develop after the flowers appear from late summer to early winter. The distinctive, musk-scented flowers are formed of six strap-like petals, candy to deep pink, rarely white, darker at the midrib, with wavy margins and usually twisted at their ends. They are borne in heads of up to eight flowers, at the end of stiff stems up to 60cm/2ft long.

Far left: The striking flowers occur in a variety of pink hues.

Right: Wild plants usually flower before the leaves appear. Those in cultivation may have both at the same time.

OTHER AMARYLIS FAMILY SPECIES

Hoop-petticoat Daffodil
Narcissus bulbocodium
This diminutive narcissus occurs naturally in Spain, Portugal, south-west France and Africa, and is commonly known as the hoop-petticoat daffodil because of the shape of its flowers. It is found on wet moors, meadows and marshes up to 1,000m/3,300ft, flowering in early to mid-spring.

Blood Lily *Haemanthus coccinea*
This is a very variable, summer-flowering bulbous perennial, occurring in widely varying habitats, mainly coastal scrub and rocky slopes, throughout the winter rainfall region of South Africa, from southern Namibia south. The flowerheads usually emerge before the leaves.

Amaryllis belladonna
Growing in the south-western Cape, *Amaryllis belladonna* has large clusters of up to 12 scented, trumpet-shaped, pink or white flowers, carried on a long purplish-red and green 50cm/20in stem in autumn. The strap-like leaves are deciduous and are produced after flowering.

Winter Daffodil *Sternbergia lutea*
With flowers up to 5cm/2in long and often as wide, of bright clear yellow, this species has long been a garden favourite, a fact that has contributed to its depletion in the wild. It once grew wild in Mediterranean regions from Spain to Iran and into Russia, but is now much reduced in number.

Sea Daffodil

Pancratium maritimum

An exotic member of the amaryllis family, the sea daffodil grows in coastal sand and dunes around the Mediterranean coastline and the Black Sea. Its sweetly and strongly scented, large white blooms are produced in summer and autumn, their six petals framing the corolla in the manner of a daffodil, *Narcissus* species, hence its common name. The plant reproduces vegetatively and through seeds, but despite the high number of seeds it produces, this method of reproduction is limited.

Identification: The fleshy, grey-green, strap-like leaves grow up to 50cm/20in long, and a long, partially flattened flower stem, to 40cm/16in, supports the inflorescence of five to ten florets, embraced before blooming by two large, skinny sepals. Large, white, fragrant blooms, up to 16cm/6½in across, with a slender, white perianth tube to 7.5cm/3in long, appear between late summer and mid-autumn. The fruit is a large, three-valved capsule.

Distribution: South-west Europe.
Height and spread: 40cm/16in.
Habit and form: Deciduous to semi-evergreen bulbous perennial.
Leaf shape: Linear.
Pollinated: Insect.

Right: The seed capsules still retain the remains of the flower.

Below: The clump-forming habit makes the flowers conspicuous among coastal dune grasses.

WATER LILIES, CAPE PONDWEEDS AND CATTAILS

Nymphaeaceae, or water lilies, are aquatic plants with showy flowers and are often considered the most primitive flowering plants. The Aponogetonaceae (cape pondweeds) are also primitive, occurring in the "Old World". The Typhaceae, or cattail family, are widespread in the Northern Hemisphere.

Water Hawthorn

Cape pondweed, *Aponogeton distachyos*

Water hawthorn occurs naturally in the winter rainfall areas of the South African Cape region, where the edible flowers and buds, which have a strong vanilla scent, are a popular winter delicacy. It is adapted to growing in ponds and small lakes that dry up in summer. The plant flowers freely in the spring, then the tubers lie dormant in the sediment, sprouting and flowering again as soon as the pools fill in autumn. The long, oval leaves float on the water, but it is usually the sweetly scented white flowers, standing up out of the water above the leaves, that attract attention. There are several other species of *Aponogeton* in southern Africa, but *A. distachyos* is the best known.

Distribution: South Africa.
Height and spread: Variable spread.
Habit and form: Aquatic perennial.
Leaf shape: Oblong-lanceolate.
Pollinated: Bee.

Identification: Oblong to lance-shaped, bright green, sometimes brown, floating leaves, up to 20cm/8in long, on long stems, are evergreen except where water dries up seasonally. Small, scented, one-petalled white flowers, 3cm/1¼in across, with purplish-brown anthers, are enclosed in white spathes, to 2cm/¾in long, and borne in racemes with forked branches, 10cm/4in long, above the water surface.

Right: The floating leaves and sweetly scented showy white flowers make this a striking water plant.

Reedmace

Bulrush, common cattail, *Typha latifolia*

This stately water reed is well known, chiefly because of its huge distribution: it is found almost worldwide, in North and Central America, Eurasia, Africa, New Zealand, Australia and Japan. The reedmace is instantly identifiable by its tall, sword-shaped leaves and distinctive fruiting spikes. It is mainly found in shallow water up to 15cm/6in deep in ponds, lakes, ditches and slow-flowing streams, and is equally tolerant of acid or alkaline conditions.

Identification: This tall, erect semi-aquatic plant grows from stout rhizomes up to 75cm/30in long, just below the soil surface. The pale greyish-green leaves are basal, erect, linear, flat, D-shaped in cross section, 1–3m/3–10ft tall; 12–16 leaves arise from each shoot. The flower stem is erect, 1.5–3m/5–10ft tall, tapering near the flower structure, which appears in midsummer. It is a dense, dark brown, cylindrical spike on the end of the stem, with the male part positioned above the female part, continuous or slightly separated.

Right: The tall flower spikes of reedmace are a familiar sight across much of the Northern Hemisphere.

Distribution: North and Central America, Eurasia, Africa, New Zealand, Australia and Japan.
Height and spread: 1.5–3m/5–10ft; indefinite spread.
Habit and form: Semi-aquatic or aquatic rhizomatous perennial.
Leaf shape: Linear.
Pollinated: Wind.

Right: The tight brown seedheads separate into a woolly mass of seed in late winter.

Prickly Water Lily

Foxnut, *Euryale ferox*

Distribution: East Asia.
Height and spread:
Variable spread.
Habit and form: Aquatic
perennial.
Leaf shape: Circular.
Pollinated: Insect.

The prickly water lily, the only species in the genus *Euryale*, is native to east Asia and China to northern India, where it may often be found in warm water ponds and lakes in lowland regions. It is quite closely related to the Amazonian giant water lily, *Victoria amazonica*: although it is not as large as that species, its leaves can be as much as 1.5m/5ft across, with bright purple undersides, laced with large veins and covered with spines. It is day-flowering, although the flower almost always opens underwater and self-pollinates before it opens.

Identification: A deep-water aquatic perennial with floating, rounded leaves, 60–150cm/2–5ft across, which are puckered, sparsely spiny, olive green above and purple beneath, with prominent, prickly veins. Shuttlecock-like flowers, up to 6cm/2¼in across, are produced in summer, with an inner row of white petals and an outer row of (usually) deep violet petals. Many-seeded, prickly berries, 5–7.5cm/2–3in across, follow the flowers. Nearly every part of the plant is covered with needle-sharp spines.

OTHER WATER LILY, CAPE PONDWEED
AND CATTAIL SPECIES

Yellow Water Lily *Nuphar lutea*
Known as brandy bottle, and widely distributed across Eurasia, north Africa, the eastern USA and the West Indies. It is often found in deeper, cooler bodies of water, where it forms dense mats on the surface. The globe-shaped, unpleasant smelling flowers are fly-pollinated and followed by decorative seedheads.

European White Water Lily *Nymphaea alba*
The white water lily is widely distributed across Eurasia and North Africa, mostly in water up to 1.2m/4ft deep, in marshes, ponds, slow-moving streams, lakes and canals. It is well known for the large, semi-double, white, faintly fragrant flowers it produces in mid- to late summer.

Dwarf Reedmace *Typha minima*
This miniature bulrush is a slender aquatic perennial, relatively common across Europe and western Asia. It is smaller than its larger relatives, reaching just 75cm/2½ft, and although the flower spikes are similar to those of the other species, the plant is much less robust and invasive.

Nymphaea candida
This large, white-flowered water lily, commonly found in ponds, lakes and slow-flowing streams in Europe and parts of north Asia, flowers from mid- to late summer. The flowers last a day, opening early and beginning to close by the afternoon; they are pollinated by flies.

Cape Blue Water Lily

Nymphaea capensis

The Cape blue water lily's star-shaped, pale blue flowers are a common sight in freshwater lakes, ponds, ditches, canals, marshes and slow-moving streams across much of east and southern Africa, as well as Madagascar. This species is widely believed to be the same as the Egyptian blue lotus, *Nymphaea caerulea*, although it is in fact not a lotus but a tropical, day-blooming water lily. Wall paintings on ancient Egyptian monuments show that this flower was venerated as a symbol of life, and was used as a euphoric and aphrodisiac.

Identification: An aquatic perennial with a thick rhizome. The mid-green leaves, arising from the rhizome, are alternate and spirally arranged, simple, rounded and toothed, with a wavy margin, 25–40cm/10–16in across, with slightly overlapping lobes, usually floating. The young leaves are purple-spotted beneath. Star-shaped, solitary flowers, 20–25cm/8–10in across, on long stalks, open during the day; they are highly fragrant, with four greenish sepals, numerous blue petals and yellow stamens. The flowers grow large when in deep water.

Distribution: Africa and Madagascar.
Height and spread: Variable.
Habit and form: Aquatic perennial.
Leaf shape: Rounded.
Pollinated: Insect.

Below: Striking blue flowers rise from beneath the water surface.

GRASSES, RUSHES AND SEDGES

The Poaceae, more commonly known as the grass family, are one of the largest families of flowering plants. The Juncaceae, or rush family, is a rather small monocot-flowering plant family. Many of these slow-growing plants superficially resemble grasses, but are herbs or woody shrubs. The Cyperaceae are grass-like, herbaceous plants, collectively called sedges, found in wet or saturated conditions.

Papyrus

Cyperus papyrus

Papyrus is native to wet swamps and lake margins throughout Africa, Madagascar and the Mediterranean region, and in particular Egypt and Sudan. The most conspicuous feature of the plant is its bright green, smooth, flowering stems, known as culms, each topped by an almost spherical cluster of thin, bright green, shiny stalks. Papyrus is famed as the fibre used by the ancient Egyptians to make paper.

Identification: The stems are stout, smooth, triangular in cross-section, 4cm/1½in thick at the base, surrounded at the base by large, leathery, tapering sheaths. They are topped by umbels of numerous, needle-like rays, 10–45cm/4–18in long, each surrounded at the base with a narrow, brown, cylindrical bract, up to 3cm/1¼in long. Greenish-brown clusters of 6–16 flowers appear at the end of the rays, followed by tiny dark brown fruits, borne in the axils of tiny scales.

Distribution: Africa and Madagascar.
Height and spread: 5m/16ft.
Habit and form: Aquatic perennial.
Leaf shape: Reduced to small bracts.
Pollinated: Wind.

Far left: Papyrus is a tall, robust, almost leafless aquatic perennial, growing from stout horizontal rhizomes that creep along the substrate under water and are anchored by numerous roots.

Giant Reed

Arundo donax

This large perennial grass is native from the Mediterranean region to the lower Himalayas, although its popularity as a garden plant has led to it being introduced to many subtropical and warm temperate regions, where it often becomes naturalized as a garden escapee and can be invasive. Giant reed is found on sand dunes near seashores and does tolerate some salt, although it is most often encountered along riverbanks and in other wet places, usually on poor sandy soil and in sunny situations, where its tough, fibrous roots penetrate deeply into the soil. Reeds for musical instruments are made from its culms.

Identification: Culms up to 6m/20ft tall arise from thick, short, branched, fleshy rhizomes. The stems are 2–4cm/¾–1½in in diameter, smooth, hollow and reed-like, with many nodes and often with a white scurf. The numerous, smooth, flat leaves on the main stem are 30–70cm/12–28in long, glaucous-green, drooping, rounded at the base and tapering to a fine point; they emerge from smooth sheaths, hairy tufted at the base. The flowers appear in mid- to late autumn in large, erect feathery panicles, 30–70cm/12–28in long, light brown or yellowish-brown, with lustrous silky hairs.

Distribution: Mediterranean to lower Himalayas.
Height and spread: Up to 6m/20ft.
Habit and form: Perennial grass.
Leaf shape: Linear.
Pollinated: Wind.

Left: The architectural merits of this plant have led to its use as a garden plant

Right: The tall stems are topped with a feathery flower panicle.

OTHER GRASSES, RUSHES AND SEDGES

Common Rush *Juncus effusus*
Common or soft rush is a long-lived perennial, wetland plant that grows in a tussock. It spreads by vigorous, underground rhizomes. It is found all over the temperate world, growing in acid or polluted soil in situations with plenty of water and sun. The bright green, hollow stems carry compact, brown or yellow flowers in summer.

Giant Feather Grass
Stipa gigantea
This grass from Spain and Portugal grows up to 1.8m/6ft tall and blooms early in summer. The flowering stems are strong and erect, and their alleged resemblance to oats, *Avena* species, gives the plant its other name of golden oats. The arching foliage is much shorter and forms a tidy clump.

Broadleaf Bamboo
Sasa palmata
This bamboo is originally native to forests in east Asia, although it has become widely naturalized in woodlands and damp hollows elsewhere. It is evergreen  and fast growing, with large leaves arranged in a fan or palm-like shape, which eventually form a dense, spreading clump.

Greater Woodrush

Luzula sylvatica

The genus name of the greater woodrush, *Luzula*, is derived from the Latin word meaning "glow worm". It probably alludes to the way that the soft, downy hairs covering the margins of each blade catch and hold dew, causing them to glisten in the morning light. It is these downy hairs that distinguish woodrushes from rushes, *Juncus* species. Woodrushes are common in temperate regions worldwide, and this Eurasian species is found in woods and shady places, as well as on open ground. The leaves remain green(ish) all winter, and in mountainous regions in western Europe they are used by most golden eagles to line their eyries. It is widely distributed in southern, western and central Europe, and south-west Asia.

Identification: Densely tufted, grass-like, tussock-forming, the greater woodrush has broadly linear, channelled, glossy, dark green leaves to 30cm/12in long, fringed with zigzagged white hairs along the margin. Groups of two to five small, chestnut-brown flowers are produced in open panicles to 7.5cm/3in long, from mid-spring to early summer.

Distribution: Europe and south-west Asia.
Height and spread: 70–80cm/28–32in.
Habit and form: Evergreen rhizomatous perennial.
Leaf shape: Broadly linear.
Pollinated: Wind.

Right: The open, feathery flower-heads emerge from mid-spring onward.

Metake

Arrow bamboo, *Pseudosasa japonica* syn. *Arundinaria japonica*

This woodland-dwelling bamboo from eastern Asia is frequently naturalized outside its range due to its popularity with gardeners. It is the most cold-tolerant bamboo, surviving temperatures as low as -24°C/-11°F. Plants often flower lightly for a number of years, although they can produce an abundance of flowers. Mass flowering severely weakens the plants, and they can take some years to recover.

Identification: An upright, spreading, bamboo up to 6m/20ft in height. The canes are erect, cylindrical, branched at each upper node, olive-green when young, maturing to pale beige. Lance-shaped or oblong, hairless, tessellated, dark green leaves, to 35cm/14in long, are silver-grey beneath and have yellow midribs. The plant usually forms a solid vertical mass of leaves, which cover and enclose it entirely from the ground to the top.

Distribution: East Asia.
Height and spread: Up to 6m/20ft.
Habit and form: Rhizomatous evergreen bamboo.
Leaf shape: Lanceolate or oblong.
Pollinated: Wind.

Right: The tiny flowers are borne at the branch tips and only appear on mature plants.

LILY FAMILY

The Liliaceae, or lily family, is a large and complex group, mostly consisting of herbaceous perennials that grow from starchy rhizomes, corms, or bulbs. The family includes a great number of ornamental flowers as well as several important agricultural crops. The plants have linear leaves, mostly with parallel veins, and flower parts in threes.

English Bluebell

Hyacinthoides non-scriptus

This bulbous perennial is restricted to northern Europe and is chiefly found in the British Isles and along the sea coasts of Scandinavia and the Low Countries, where it thrives in the cool, moist, maritime conditions. It grows in deciduous woodland, where it carpets the ground, usually on slightly acid soils, and is also common in woodland clearings, on roadsides and occasionally in open ground. The distinct species is also threatened in many areas across its range because it hybridizes freely with the Spanish bluebell, *H. hispanica*, which is a more robust species.

Left: The flowers are distinct.

Identification: The plant is vigorous and clump-forming, with spreading, linear to lance-shaped, glossy, dark green leaves, 20–45cm/8–18in long. In spring, one-sided racemes that bend over at the top bear 6–12 pendent, narrowly bell-shaped, scented, mid-blue, sometimes white, flowers, up to 2cm/¾in long, with cream anthers. Blooms appear (according to local climate and conditions) from mid- to late spring.

Right: Bluebells seed easily.

Far right: Bluebells formdense blue carpets during spring in deciduous woodlands.

Distribution: Northern Europe.
Height and spread: 20–45cm/8–18in.
Habit and form: Bulbous perennial.
Leaf shape: Linear to lanceolate.
Pollinated: Insect.

Madonna Lily

Lilium candidum

A large upright lily and one of the oldest plants recorded, being recognizable in paintings on Crete dating back 4,000 years. It has been cultivated for centuries and its original habitat (probably Turkey) is unknown, although it now occurs widely across that region. It is highly unusual in that it produces overwintering basal leaves. It grows in meadows and forests on sand and limestone, to elevations of 1,300m/4,250ft.

Identification: Broad, inversely lance-shaped, shiny, bright green basal leaves, 23cm/9in long, appear in autumn. In spring, the stiffly erect stems bear smaller, scattered or spirally arranged, often somewhat twisted, lance-shaped leaves to 7.5cm/3in long. From late spring until midsummer the plant produces a raceme of 5–20 sweetly fragrant, large, broadly trumpet-shaped, pure white flowers, 5–7.5cm/2–3in long, with yellowish bases and bright yellow anthers.

Left and right: The flower spikes sport 10–20 dazzling white, sweetly scented flowers in summer.

Distribution: Mediterranean.
Height and spread: 1–1.8m/3–6ft.
Habit and form: Bulbous perennial.
Leaf shape: Inversely lanceolate.
Pollinated: Insect.

Pineapple Lily

Eucomis bicolor

These bulbous perennials, originating from wet mountain slopes and meadows in South Africa, are named pineapple lilies because of their unusual tight racemes of flowers topped by a small tuft of leafy bracts, similar to those of a pineapple, which are borne in late summer. These emerge amid a basal rosette of glossy green leaves and are borne on stout stems, giving the whole plant a highly distinctive look.

Far right: The individual flowerhead.

Left: The exotic-looking flowerheads resemble pineapples.

Identification: A large bulb, up to 7.5cm/3in in diameter, produces semi-erect to angular, strap-shaped, wavy-margined, light green leaves, growing up to 10cm/4in wide and 30–50cm/12–20in long. In late summer, maroon-flecked stems bear racemes, 15cm/6in long, of tightly packed, slightly pendent, pale green flowers up to 2.5cm/1in across, with purple-margined tepals. Each raceme is topped by a small tuft of leafy bracts, arranged in a loose rosette.

Right: The rosette of leaves gives rise to a single flower stem.

Distribution: South Africa.
Height and spread: 30–60cm/12–24in.
Habit and form: Bulbous perennial.
Leaf shape: Angular strap-shaped.
Pollinated: Insect.

OTHER LILY FAMILY SPECIES

Snakeshead Fritillary
Fritillaria meleagris
Native to north-western Europe, the snakeshead fritillary usually grows in damp meadows. The bloom, before the bud is fully opened, looks a little like a snake's head, hence the name. The nodding, tulip-shaped flowers are chequered in shades of purple or, rarely, white.

Yellow Asphodel *Asphodeline lutea*
A native of the eastern Mediterranean, yellow asphodel is a clump-forming evergreen perennial, with tightly wrapped, blade-like, narrowly triangular foliage. Tall flowering spikes, which become dense with fragrant, citron-yellow, star-shaped blooms, emerge in spring.

Toad Lily *Tricyrtris stolonifera*
The toad lily is a stoloniferous perennial from moist woodland habitats in Taiwan. It has purple-spotted, deep green leaves, borne alternately on hairy stems that grow in a zigzag pattern. In late summer, it bears white or light pink, star-shaped flowers, heavily spotted with purple.

Oriental Lily *Lilium speciosum*
This tall Japanese lily can reach 1.5m/5ft and flowers late in the summer. The large, pendent, sweetly fragrant, white flowers are borne on long racemes of 12 or more, and are covered in carmine-red spots and stripes, giving them a pink appearance.

Water Lily Tulip

Tulipa kaufmanniana

This relatively low-growing tulip, from rocky mountain slopes close to the snow edge in central Asia, has an average height of 15cm/6in, though it is a variable species in terms of height and bloom. The flower is long and white with a yellow tint on the inside and pink on the outside. The blooms, when they first open, are cup-shaped, though with pointed petals; eventually, on the sunniest days, they open flat into a characteristic hexagonal star shape from about a third of the way up the slender cup, so that when viewed from above they look almost like water lilies. The species has a scattered distribution across Kazakhstan, Uzbekistan, Tajikistan and Kyrgyzstan.

Identification: The plant has three to five lance-shaped, slightly wavy-margined, hairless, grey-green leaves, up to 25cm/10in long. Bowl-shaped flowers 3–12.5cm/1¼–5in across, are borne singly or in clusters of up to five, on slightly downy, often red-tinged stems in early and mid-spring. The flowers are cream or yellow, flushed pink or greyish-green on the outside, often with contrasting basal marks.

Distribution: Central Asia.
Height and spread: 15cm/6in.
Habit and form: Bulbous perennial.
Leaf shape: Lanceolate.
Pollinated: Insect.

Right: Tulips escape the extremes of summer heat and winter cold as an underground bulb.

Below: Bulbs may form dense clumps over time.

TERRESTRIAL ORCHIDS

The Orchidaceae, or orchid family, are terrestrial, epiphytic or saprophytic herbs comprising one of the two largest families of flowering plants, with about 1,000 genera and 15–20,000 species. The terrestrial species often display ingenious relationships with their pollinators, and although the flowers are generally smaller than some of the epiphytic types they are equally intricate.

Lady's Slipper

Cypripedium calceolus

This orchid, with large, solitary flowers with maroon-brown petals and a pouched, yellow lip, is found in open woodlands on calcareous soils, usually on north-facing slopes. It is widely distributed throughout Europe, and eastward across Asia to the Pacific coast and on into much of northern North America. There are several varieties across the range with different flower sizes to accommodate different pollinators. Despite this wide distribution, however, over-collection has made it rare and threatened over much of its range even though efforts have been made to protect it.

Identification: This terrestrial orchid has three to five oval to elliptic leaves, ascending, sheathing at the base, with pointed to tapered tips, sparsely hairy, 5–20cm/2–8in long. The stem is 40cm/16in tall, hairy, the hairs often glandular. Flowers are usually borne one per stem, less often two, in early to midsummer. The sepals and lateral petals are greenish-yellow to purplish-brown, 2–6cm/¾–2¼in long, the upper sepal lance-shaped to oval, the lateral sepals joined below the lip, the lateral petals narrowly lance-shaped and twisted. The lip is yellow, often purple-veined and dotted with purple around the orifice, and heavily pouched in the style of a slipper.

Distribution: Eurasia and North America.
Height and spread: 40cm/16in.
Habit and form: Herbaceous perennial.
Leaf shape: Ovate to elliptic.
Pollinated: Insect.

Bee Orchid

Ophrys apifera

Bee orchids, although not particularly rare across their range, are unpredictable in their appearance, often varying hugely in numbers from year to year. This is probably due to the plant's habit of overwintering as a dormant tuber. Dry years reduce the size of the orchids, resulting in the plant not flowering for a year or more after. It is a frequently encountered species of limestone grasslands, old limestone quarries, maquis and sand dunes and is typically found in areas of short, grazed turf across Europe ranging eastward into northern Asia. The flower mimics the female of a Mediterranean bee species to attract potential "suitors" who attempt to mate with it. When a male bee lands on the flower, pollen is dumped on its back and it flies off with this to cross-fertilize another flower. Despite this intricacy, many northern populations are self-pollinating as the bee is absent in their location.

Identification: An erect, perennial, terrestrial orchid, with small rosettes of oblong to egg-shaped leaves, 6cm/2¼in long, pointed at the tip, appearing early in the year. Erect racemes, up to 30cm/12in tall, of 2–11 flowers, 2.5cm/1in across, each with green or purplish-pink sepals and petals, and a brownish furry lip marked red-purple and yellow, which is supposed to resemble a bee, are borne in mid-spring and early summer.

Distribution: Europe and northern Asia.
Height and spread: 30cm/12in.
Habit and form: Herbaceous perennial.
Leaf shape: Oblong-ovate.
Pollinated: Bee.

Left: The bee orchid gets its name for its ability to attract male solitary bees to its flowers.

Pride of Table Mountain

Disa uniflora

Distribution: Western Cape, South Africa.
Height and spread: Up to 60cm/2ft.
Habit and form: Herbaceous perennial.
Leaf shape: Lanceolate.
Pollinated: Butterfly (*Meneris tulbaghia*).

Far right: The bright red flowers appear in clusters.

Disa is a large African genus and, although widespread, many species are endemic to small areas. The spectacular, brilliant red flowers of *D. uniflora*, which are the emblem of the Western Cape, are borne during summer and are found in fynbos, on rock flushes, in marshes and lakes, and in montane grassland. It is always associated with water, growing on the edges of permanent mountain streams or in wet moss near waterfalls, at altitudes varying from sea level to about 1,200m/4,000ft. The butterfly, *Meneris tulbaghia*, is the only known pollinator, although the plant readily multiplies by producing stolons that develop into new plants. After flowering, the plant and its tuber die back to provide food for the production of a fresh tuber and shoot.

Identification: A deciduous terrestrial orchid, with lance-shaped leaves up to 25cm/10in long, it produces short racemes of up to three, or rarely up to ten, brilliant scarlet flowers, each 7.5–12.5cm/3–5in across, with hooded upper perianth and spreading lower perianth segments. The hood is paler with darker red striations; the lower twin petals have a green stripe on the outer surface. The bud is tightly curled and upward facing.

OTHER TERRESTRIAL ORCHID SPECIES

Man Orchid *Aceras anthropophorum*
The man orchid has a patchy distribution, ranging from the Mediterranean region to Turkey, but is much reduced over its former range due to grassland disturbance. The yellowish flowers resemble small human figures, with the upper flower parts forming a "helmet".

Pyramidal Orchid
Anacamptis pyramidalis
This orchid is so-called because of the obvious rounded-pyramid shape of the flowering spike, especially when young. The flowers are a beautiful deep pink, with a short spur; they have a faint fragrance and are moth-pollinated. The leaves are narrow and without any spots.

Satyrium princeps
This South African terrestrial orchid is a native of fynbos regions, especially in coastal districts. It has heads of scented white flowers that emerge from broad, flat basal foliage. It is extremely rare in the wild, with only scattered populations around the southern Cape.

Cypripedium himalaicum
Found from northern Europe east to northern Asia and Siberia, this orchid grows on thin, stony soils in open woodland clearings, up to and sometimes over 3,000m/9,850ft. In the late spring and early summer, waxy, brittle flowers that are pink, red and white appear on an erect, single-flowered inflorescence.

Early Purple Orchid

Orchis mascula

The early purple orchid is a widespread but local plant of woods, hedge banks, pasture and low coastal cliffs. It is very common on lime-rich or clay soils, particularly in warm, moist areas close to the coast. It is relatively common across Europe, in oak groves, undergrowth, meadows and on roadsides, up to a maximum elevation of 2,400m/8,000ft. The leaves are often marked with dark spots, and although purple is the most common colour a white variant is occasionally encountered. The production of seed often heralds the death of the plant.

Identification: A terrestrial orchid with roots consisting of roundish tubers, from which arise erect, mid-green, often purple-spotted leaves 15cm/6in long. From spring to midsummer it bears light to dark purple flowers, 2cm/¾in long, in erect racemes to 30cm/12in tall. The lowest petal is three-lobed with a stout spur, wider than the bracts. The flowers have a mild vanilla-like aroma.

Distribution: Europe except Iceland.
Height and spread: 30cm/12in.
Habit and form: Herbaceous perennial.
Leaf shape: Oblong-ovate.
Pollinated: Bee and moth.

Below: True to its name the early purple orchid flowers earlier than other orchids.

EPIPHYTIC AND LITHOPHYTIC ORCHIDS

These orchids depend upon the support of another plant, though they are not parasitic. They typically root into accumulations of plant debris in the forks of tree branches and manufacture their own food by photosynthesis. They are generally forest dwellers, many conducting their entire life cycles elevated in their host trees or on inaccessible rocky outcrops. They include some of the showiest of all flowers.

Dendrobium aphyllum

These deciduous, tropical, epiphytic orchids are widespread in South-east Asia, being found in low-altitude rainforests right up into montane forests. The large pale mauve and primrose yellow flowers have a strong violet fragrance and are borne from stem-like pseudobulbs before the new leaves appear. The foliage has a soft texture and is typically deciduous after a single season, though under some conditions leaves may last more than a single year.

Identification: Pendent to semi-erect, long, slender pseudobulbs are slightly swollen at the nodes, with new growths appearing about flowering time. Oval, fleshy leaves, 12.5cm/5in long, often wavy along the margin, are often smaller near the tips of the canes. Pale mauve-pink flowers, 5cm/2in across, with primrose-yellow lips, are borne in pairs, emerging from nodes along the previous season's leafless growth, and are so numerous that the canes appear covered with blossoms.

Above: The leaves are fleshy.

Right: The flowerhead is spectacular.

Distribution: South-east Asia from southern and eastern India to south-west China, Thailand, Laos, Vietnam, Malaysia and South Andaman Island.
Height and spread: 60–180cm/2–6ft, trailing.
Habit and form: Deciduous epiphyte.
Leaf shape: Ovate to lanceolate.
Pollinated: Insect.

Four Season Orchid

Corsage orchid, *Cymbidium ensifolium*

This lithophytic orchid is one of the most widespread and variable of the genus. It is found throughout South-east Asia, growing at elevations from 300–1,800m/1,000–5,900ft. It has many distinct recognized subtypes, which some experts believe constitute several closely related species, although most consider it a single species throughout its range.

Left and right: The large, showy flowers of this orchid emerge from among the mass of tufted, grass-like leaves during the summer months.

Identification: This plant has small, ovoid pseudobulbs, often hidden from view, clumped along a short rhizome that gives rise to thick, white, branching roots. The persistent, linear, tufted, grass-like leaves are up to 30cm/12in long, sometimes with minutely serrated tips. In summer, it produces upright racemes of 3–12 waxy, greenish-yellow flowers, each 2.5–5cm/1–2in across, with spreading sepals and petals streaked with red. Green or pale yellow, rarely white, lips, with wavy margins and callus ridges converging at the apex and forming a tube at mid-lobe base, are irregularly spotted red-brown.

Distribution: Indochina, China, Japan, Borneo, New Guinea and the Philippines.
Height and spread: 30cm/12in.
Habit and form: Lithophytic orchid.
Leaf shape: Linear.
Pollinated: Insect.

Moth Orchid

Phalaenopsis amabilis

Distribution: Philippines.
Height and spread: Up to 90cm/3ft.
Habit and form: Epiphyte.
Leaf shape: Obovate-oblong.
Pollinated: Insect.

This robust epiphytic orchid from the Philippines is very variable, occurring at elevations up to 600m/2,000ft on the trunks and branches of rainforest trees, overhanging rivers, swamps and streams. The short, stem-like rhizome gives rise to long, shiny leaves, among which the spectacular, large, scented, white flowers are borne along pendent racemes and may persist for many weeks before dropping. This is one of the national flowers of Indonesia.

Identification: The short, robust stem is completely enclosed by overlapping leaf-sheaths. The long, fleshy, smooth, often branched, flexible roots are green at the end. The glossy leaves, seldom more than five, are fleshy or leathery, oval to oblong and blunt-tipped, up to 50cm/20in long. Pendent, simple or branched racemes, up to 90cm/3ft long, ascending or arched, green dotted brown-purplish, bear numerous white, often fragrant flowers, with yellow-margined lips and red throat margins, 6–10cm/2¼–4in across.

Below: The large white flowers of the moth orchid are sweetly scented and often persist for months, high in the rainforest canopy.

OTHER EPIPHYTIC ORCHID SPECIES
Dendrobium densiflorum
This epiphytic orchid from India has bunches of showy, fragrant blooms on pendent, very densely flowered racemes that may reach 25cm/10in or more, arising from near the base of the stem. The lip of the flower is bright orange, with the rest of the flower paler yellow-orange.

Blue Orchid *Vanda coerulea*
With its white or pale blue flowers dramatically marked with purple, this north Indian orchid's spectacular and unusual blooms are popular with orchid enthusiasts. As a consequence large numbers have been stripped from the wild. Today it is rare and its habitat is under threat.

Angel Orchid *Coelogyne cristata*
This orchid is from the Himalayas, where it grows in cool mountain regions that experience dry cool winters and heavy rainfall during monsoon months. The pure crystalline-white flowers, up to 7.5cm/3in across, with a lip that has a deep yolk-yellow crest, grow in groups of three to ten per stem.

Bulbophyllum medusae
This unusual South-east Asian orchid, found from Thailand to Borneo and the Philippines, is named after the snake-haired gorgon Medusa of Greek mythology because of its strange, fringed flowers, with lateral sepals that grow to 12.5cm/5in long. The arching umbels of flowers emerge from the base of the pseudobulbs.

Scorpion Orchid

Air-flower arachnis, *Arachnis flos-aeris*

All *Arachnis* orchids are known as scorpion orchids, but the name is especially applied to this species. Mainly a lowland plant that inhabits more open areas in full sun, this is not strictly an epiphyte but a vining, monopodial orchid. It can be found scrambling over rocks and trees, usually at elevations up to 1,000m/3,300ft in wet tropical forests of South-east Asia. It is a large species, which will climb high into the treetops if given the opportunity.

Identification: It has a thick, robust stem that roots adventitiously on to supporting plants and thick, fleshy or leathery, dark green leaves, 18cm/7in long and notched at the tips. The fragrant flowers, up to 10cm/4in across with a fixed lip and four pollinia, are yellow-green horizontally striped or spotted maroon, or in shades of yellow to gold with red-brown markings. They are borne in arching, axillary panicles or racemes, pendent or ascending, up to 1.8m/6ft long, with many flowers that open over a long period.

Distribution: Thailand, western Malaysia and the Philippines.
Height and spread: 6m/20ft or more.
Habit and form: Climbing orchid.
Leaf shape: Obovate-oblong.
Pollinated: Insect.

Above: The huge inflorescences have showy flowers that gradually open along their length.

GLOSSARY

Annual a plant which completes its entire life-cycle within a year.

Anther the pollen-bearing portion of the stamen.

Areole elevation on a cactus stem, bearing a spine.

Axil the upper angle between an axis and any off-shoot or lateral organ arising from it, especially a leaf.

Axillary situated in, or arising from, or pertaining to an axil.

Basal leaf arising from the rootstock or a very short or buried stem.

Beak a long, pointed, horn-like projection; particularly applied to the terminal points of fruits and pistils.

Beaked furnished with a beak.

Beard (on flower) a tuft or zone of hair as on the falls of bearded irises.

Berry indehiscent (non-drying) fruit, one- to many-seeded; the product of a single pistil. Frequently misapplied to any pulpy or fleshy fruit regardless of its constitution.

Biennial lasting for two seasons from germination to death, generally blooming in the second season.

Boss-like (of the standard) Taking on the appearance of a boss (round metal stud in the centre of a shield or ornamental work).

Bract a modified protective leaf associated with the inflorescence (clothing the stalk and subtending the flowers), with buds and with newly emerging shoots.

Branched rootstock a branching underground stem.

Bromeliad a type of South American plant predominantly found growing on other plants but not parasitically.

Calcicole a plant dwelling on and favouring calcareous (lime-rich) soils.

Calcifuge a plant avoiding and damaged by calcareous soils.

Callus ridge (calli) superficial protuberances on the lip of many orchid flowers.

Capsule (of fruit) a dry (dehiscent) seed vessel.

Carpet-forming with a dense, ground-hugging habit; hence "carpet-like".

Cauline (of leaves) attached to or arising from the stem.

Chlorophyll green pigment that facilitates food production, is present in most plants.

Cleistogamous with self-pollination occurring in the closed flower.

Climbing habit any plant that climbs or has a tendency to do so, usually by means of various adaptations of stems, leaves or roots.

Clubbed spur a tubular or sac-like basal extension of a flower, generally projecting backward and containing nectar, gradually thickening upward from a slender base.

Clump-forming forming a tight mass of close-growing stems or leaves at or near ground level.

Column (of the flower) a feature of orchids, where the style and stamens are fused together in a single structure.

Composite (of flowers and leaves) a single leaf or petal divided in such a way as to resemble many.

Compound (of flowers and leaves) divided into two or more subsidiary parts.

Contractile roots roots which contract in length and pull parts of a plant further into the soil.

Convex petal with an outline or shape like that of the exterior of a sphere.

Cordate heart-shaped.

Cormous perennial a plant or stem base living for two or more years with a solid, swollen, subterranean, bulb-like stem.

Corolla a floral envelope composed of free or fused petals.

Corona a crown or cup-like appendage or ring of appendages.

Corymb an indeterminate flat-topped or convex inflorescence, where the outer flowers open first.

Creeping habit trailing on or under the

surface, and sometimes rooting.

Culms the stems of grasses.

Cupped (flowers) shaped like a cup.

Curving spur a tubular or sac-like basal extension of a flower, generally projecting backward and containing nectar, being curved in shape.

Cyathia flower form, shaped like a cup.

Cylindrical follicle cylindrical elongated fruit, virtually circular in cross-section.

Cyme (flowers) a more or less flat-topped and determinate flowerhead, with the central or terminal flower opening first.

Decumbent base (of the stem) lying horizontally along the ground but with the apex ascending and almost erect.

Decurrent where the base of a leaf extends down to the petiole (if any) and the stem.

Deeply cut petals or leaves with deeply incised lobes.

Deeply segmented petals or leaves that are sharply divided into several segments.

Deltoid an equilateral triangle attached by the broad end rather than the point; shaped like the Greek letter delta.

Dilated concavity dilating, broadened, expanded, in the manner of the outer surface of a sphere.

Dioecious with male and female flowers on different plants.

Disc floret part of the central flowerhead in the Asteraceae. Short tubular florets as opposed to the peripheral ray florets.

Dissected leaf shape cut in any way; a term applicable to leaf blades or other flattened organs that are incised.

Domed flowerhead Compound flowerhead arranged in a dome shape.

Drupe a one- to several-seeded fruit, contained within a soft, fleshy, pericarp, as in stone fruits.

Ellipsoid resembling an ellipse shape.
Epidermis the outer layer of plant tissue; skin.
Epiphytic growing on plants without being parasitic.
Ericaceous in broad terms, resembling *Erica* spp. In habit, plants preferring acidic soil conditions.
Evergreen plant with foliage that remains green for at least a year, through more than one growing season.

Farinose having a mealy, granular texture on the surface.
Filament stalk that bears the anther at its tips, together forming a stamen.
Floret a very small flower, generally part of a congested inflorescence.

Genus The first name of a plant described under the binomial system of botanical naming.
Glandular bearing glands, or hairs with gland-like prominence at the tip.
Glandular inflorescence a compound flowerhead with a glandular surface.
Glycoside A compound related to sugar that plays many important roles in living organisms, with numerous plant-produced glycosides used as medications.

Hastate arrow-shaped, triangular, with two equal and approximately triangular basal lobes, pointing laterally outward rather than toward the stalk.
Haustorium a sucker in parasitic plants that penetrates the host.
Hemi-parasite only parasitic for part of its life cycle; not entirely dependent upon the host for nutrition.
Hemispheric a half sphere shape.
Herb abbreviation for herbaceous. Not the culinary herb.
Herbaceous pertaining to herbs, i.e. lacking persistent aerial parts or lacking woody parts.
Herbaceous perennial herbaceous plant living for three or more years. Referred to as herb.
Hip the fleshy, developed floral cup and the enclosed seeds of a rose.
Hooded flowers one or more petals, fused and forming a hood over the sexual reproductive parts of the flower.
Hooked spurs a tubular or sac-like basal extension of a flower, generally projecting backwards and containing nectar; being hooked in shape.

Inflorescences the arrangement of flowers and their accessory parts in multiple heads, on a central axis or stem.

Keeled (leaves) a prominent ridge, like the keel of a boat, running longitudinally down the centre of the undersurface of a leaf.

Labellum a lip, especially the enlarged or otherwise distinctive third petal of an orchid.
Layering stems rooting on contact with the earth and forming colonies of cloned plants.
Leaf
　Lobed divided into (usually rounded) segments, lobes, separated from adjacent segments.
　Toothed possessing teeth, often qualified, as saw-toothed or bluntly toothed.
　Uneven margins with one margin exceeding the one opposite.
　Wavy margin having a wavy edge.
Leaf axil the point immediately above the point of leaf attachment, often containing a bud.
Leaf tip
　pointed ending in a distinct point.
　rounded with no visible point.
Leaflet units of a compound leaf.
Lenticel elliptical and raised cellular pore on the surface of bark or the surface tissue of fruit, through which gases can penetrate.

Liana a woody climbing vine.
Lignotuber a starchy swelling on underground stems or roots, often used to survive fire or browsing animals.
Lip petal, or part thereof, which is either modified or differentiated from the others, on which insects can alight.
Lithophytic growing on rocks or stony soil, deriving nourishment from the atmosphere rather than the soil.
Low-growing plants that do not reach any significant height; ground hugging.

Membranous capsule seedpod with thin walls.
Mesic a type of habitat with a moderate or well-balanced supply of moisture, e.g. a mesic forest.
Midrib the primary vein of a leaf or leaflet, usually running down its centre as a continuation of the leaf stem.
Monocarpic dying after flowering and bearing fruit only once.
Monopedal a stem or rhizome in which growth continues indefinitely from the apical or terminal bud, and generally exhibits no secondary branching.
Monoecious A plant with both male and female flowers/flower parts on the same plant (Syn. Hermaphrodite)
Morphologically pertaining to the study of the form of plants.
Mucilage viscous substance obtained from plant seeds exposed to water.

Nectary a gland, often in the form of a protuberance or depression, which secretes and sometimes absorbs nectar.
Node the point on a stem where one or more leaves, shoots, whorls, branches or flowers are attached.

Open habit growing loosely with space between the branches.

Panicle indeterminate branched

inflorescence, the branches generally resemble racemes or corymbs.

Pea-like flowers that are like those of the pea (*Psium* spp.)

Pendent hanging downward, more markedly than arching or nodding but not as a result of the weight of the part in question or the weakness of its attachment or support.

Pendent raceme raceme inflorescence with a pendent habit.

Pendulous branch branch with a pendent habit.

Perennial a plant lasting for three seasons or more.

Perfoliate a sessile leaf of which the basal lobes are united, the stem seems to pass through the blade.

Perianth the collective term for the floral envelopes, the corolla and calyx, especially when the two are not clearly differentiated.

Perianth tube the effect of fused petals resulting in a tubular flower shape

Petaloid sepal segment that encloses the flower when in bud that resembles a true petal.

Petaloid tepal tepal that resembles a petal.

Photosynthesis the synthesis of sugar and oxygen from carbon dioxide and water, carried out by all green plants.

Pinnate feather-like; an arrangement of more than three leaflets in two rows.

Pinnatifid pinnately cleft nearly to the midrib in broad divisions, but without separating into distinct leaflets or pinnae.

Pistil the female reproductive organs of a flower consisting of one or more carpel.

Pod appendage containing seeds:
  Inflated pod fruits that are inflated and balloon like

Cylindrical pod elongated fruits, virtually circular in cross-section.
Flattened distinctly flattened along one plane.

Pinnatisect shape deeply and pinnately cut to, or near to, the midrib; the divisions, narrower than in pinnatifid, are not truly distinct segments.

Pouched bracts a modified protective leaf associated with the inflorescence and possessing a pouched shape.

Primary rays The outer petaloid rays, usually associated with a composite flower such as those in Asteraceae.

Procumbent trailing loosely or lying flat along the surface of the ground, without rooting.

Prostate lying flat on the ground.

Pseudobulb the water-storing thickened "bulb-like" stem found in many sympodial orchids.

Pseudostem not a true stem but made up of leaf sheaths.

Quadrangular stem four-angled, as in the stems of some *Passiflora* and succulent *Euphorbia* spp.

Raceme an indeterminate, un-branched and elongate inflorescence composed of flowers in stalks.

Ramicaul thin leaf stem usually associated with orchids.

Rambling habit an unruly spreading or partially climbing growth habit.

Ray floret a small flower with a tubular corolla and the limb expanded and flattened in a strap-like blade, usually occupying the outer rings of a capitulum (daisy flower).

Reflexed abruptly deflexed at more than a 90 degree angle.

Reniform kidney shaped.

Reniform scale kidney-shaped leaf scale.

Rhizome underground stem.

Rhizomatous producing or possessing rhizomes; rhizome-like.

Rhombic ovate oval to diamond-shaped; angularly oval, the base and apex forming acute angles.

Root sucker stem arising directly from the roots of a parent plant.

Rootstock the roots and stem base of a plant.

Rosette forming leaves arranged in a basal rosette or rosettes.

Runcinate a leaf, petal or petal-like structure, usually oblanceolate in outline and with sharp, prominent teeth or broad, incised lobes pointing backward toward the base, away from a generally acute apex, as in *Taraxacum* (dandelion).

Runner prostrate or recumbent stem, taking root and giving rise to a plantlet at its apex and sometimes at nodes.

Sagitate arrow- or spear-shaped, where the equal and approximately triangular basal lobes of leaves point downward or toward the stalk.

Saprophytic deriving its nutrition from dissolved or decayed organic matter.

Scalloped rounded in outline in the manner of a scallop shell.

Scape an erect, leafless stalk, supporting an inflorescence or flower.

Scrambling habit not strictly climbing but vigorous with a tendency to grow over surrounding vegetation.

Seed ripened, fertilized ovule; an embryonic plant.

Seedhead describes the fruiting bodies of a plant.

Seedpod describes the enclosing body around developing seeds.

Semipendent flowerhead only partially pendent in nature.

Sepal modified leaf-like structure, enclosing and protecting the inner floral parts prior to its opening.

Serrated toothed margin, with teeth resembling those of a saw.

Shrub a loose descriptive term for a woody plant which produces multiple stems, shoots or branches from its base, but does not have a single trunk.

Shrublet a small shrub or a dwarf, woody-based and closely branched plant.

Sickle-shaped crescent-shaped.

Single flowers with one set of petals.
Solitary flowers borne singly (i.e. not in an inflorescence).
Spadix (Spadisces pl.) a fleshy, columnar flower, often enclosed in a spathe and typical of plants in the family Araceae.
Spathe a conspicuous leaf or bract subtending a spadix or other inflorescence.
Spathulate spatula-shaped, essentially oblong, but attenuated at the base and rounded at the apex.
Species the second name used to identify a plant with particular characteristics under the binomial system of botanical naming.
Spike an indeterminate inflorescence bearing sessile flowers on an un-branched axis.
Sprawling spreading in an untidy manner.
Spreading stems or branches extending horizontally outward.
Spur a tubular or sac-like basal extension of the flower, projecting backward and often containing nectar.
Stalked a general term for the stem-like support of any organ.
Stamen the male floral organ, bearing an anther, generally on a filament, and producing pollen.
Staminode sterile stamen or stamen-like structure, often rudimentary or modified, sometimes petal-like and frequently antherless.
Standard (1) in pea flowers, the large, uppermost petal; (2) an erect or ascending unit of the inner whorl of an *Iris* flower.
Stigma the end of a pistil that receives the pollen and normally differs in texture from the rest of the style.
Stipule leafy or bract-like appendage at the base of a leaf stem, usually occurring in pairs and soon shed.

Stolon a prostrate or recumbent stem, taking root and giving rise to plantlets at its apex and sometimes at nodes.
Stoloniferous possessing stolons.
Straggly untidy, rather stretched in appearance.
Subopposite more or less opposite, but with one leaf or leaflet of a pair slightly above or below its partner.
Suborbicular more or less circular.
Subshrub a perennial with a woody base and soft shoots.
Subspecies a species further divided into distinct populations.
Succulent thickly cellular and fleshy.
Suckering shrub shrub with a tendency to produce root suckers as part of its normal growth.

Tendril a modified branch, leaf or axis, filiform, scandent, and capable of attaching itself to a support either by twining or adhesion.
Tepal perianth segment that cannot be defined as either petal or sepal.
Terminal at the tip or apex of a stem.
Terrestrial living on land; growing in the soil.
Tessellated chequered, composed of small squares as in the flower of *Fritillaria meleagris* or the intersecting vein pattern of some leaves.
Thorn sharp hard outgrowth from the stem wood.
Throat the central opening of tubular or bell-shaped flowers.
Toothed margin leaf edge possessing teeth, often qualified, as saw-toothed or bluntly toothed.
Trailing prostrate but not rooting.
Trefoil leaf divided into three leaflets.
Trifoliate three-leaved.
Tuberoid in the manner of a tuber.
Tuberous bearing tubers, tuberous-bearing tubers, or resembling a tuber.
Tulip-shaped similar shape to the flower of a tulip.
Tussock-forming forming a tight mass of close growing stems or leaves at or near ground level, with grass-like leaves.
Twining vine a climbing plant that twines around a support.
Two-lipped (flower) with two lips.

Umbellate pattern resembling an umbel.
Umbel a flat-topped inflorescence like a corymb, but with all the flowered

pedicels (rays) arising from the same point at the apex of the main axis.
Unisexual a flower that is either male or female.
Upright a flowerhead that is held vertically or nearly so.
Upright habit Growth that is vertical or nearly so.

Variety a distinct population that does not merit the status of species or sub-species in its own right.
Vein/veinlets an externally visible strand of vascular tissue.
Vestigial a leaf that was functional and fully developed in ancestral forms, but is now smaller and less developed.
Vine a general term to describe some climbing plants.

Whorl when three or more organs are arranged in a circle at one node or, loosely, around the same axis.
Woody ligneous (containing the plant protein lignin), approaching the nature of wood.

Acknowledgements
With thanks to Spillifords Wildlife Garden, Devon, and The English Cottage Garden Nursery, Kent.
The publishers would like to thank the following people and picture libraries for permission to use their images:
Ardea page 26 br, page 27tc, 29.
Garden Matters page 56, 96.
Peter Barrett page 23 bc.
Photos Horticultural page 26 bl, 72, 115.

INDEX